MANGA
FOR SUCCESS

MARKETING

AUTHOR
TAKASHI YASUDA

ARTWORK BY
ENJU SHIGEMATSU

WILEY

For general information on our other products and services or for technical support, please contact our Customer Care Department within the United States at (800) 762-2974, outside the United States at (317) 572-3993 or fax (317) 572-4002.

Wiley also publishes its books in a variety of electronic formats. Some content that appears in print may not be available in electronic formats. For more information about Wiley products, visit our website at www.wiley.com.

Library of Congress Cataloging-in-Publication Data is Available:
ISBN 9781394176137 (Paperback)
ISBN 9781394176144 (ePub)
ISBN 9781394176151 (ePDF)

Cover Design: JMA Management Center Inc.
Cover Images: JMA Management Center Inc.
© ShEd Artworks/Shutterstock

SKY10042726_032223

Contents

Part 1

What Is Marketing?

Part 2

The Pros and Cons of Viral Marketing

Part 3

Understanding the People Who Buy Your Products

Sorting out Your Company's Relationship with Your Customers

Part 5

Decide Who Your Customers Are

Part 6

Deciding Your 4 Ps

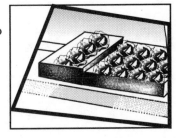

Establishing Long-Term Relationships with Your Customers

Introduction

Why did you pick up this book?

Do you want to increase your product sales? Are you interested in developing products and services that can help improve customer satisfaction? Maybe you work in retail or sales and you'd like to acquire some basic knowledge about marketing. There are probably a lot of you who are looking to learn and apply some marketing knowledge in your respective jobs.

You could also be someone who's about to start working full-time and you're thinking you'd like to learn about marketing beforehand. Maybe you're thinking that knowing about marketing will give you an edge in job interviews. You might be a student having a hard time in a marketing class and you just want a basic overview that's easy to understand. Or you might be someone looking for a book with a more practical approach to marketing instead of an academic one.

Marketing is an all-around tool that can help you become more efficient at work and improve the quality of your life.

It can lead to an increase in sales and profit which can lead to better salaries and income, improving your social standing in the long run.

Needless to say, knowledge of marketing is crucial if you have a job related to planning, business, and sales. In addition, marketing knowledge can be an advantage even for regular office work. From work procedures to presentations to everyday communication—learning about marketing offers a variety of benefits for a wide array of situations. For specialists in creative fields, marketing can help better convey the value of your skills and products, making for happier paying customers and clients.

This book was written to make marketing easier to understand with the help of practical examples and situations illustrated in manga form. To make the examples relatable to a wider range of people, the manga portions are set in a family-owned, small-town Japanese manju bun shop. Manju buns are cakes steamed with fillings such as sweet bean paste, custards, and meats. An elderly couple tries their hardest to keep their long-time business running while our heroine is someone who has grown just a little weary of her city life. Two unusual guests visit their shop and our story takes off from there. The manga is designed to give you a simulated experience of actual situations, and the analysis that follows helps you absorb marketing concepts as illustrated by the manga.

Whatever your reason for picking this book up, I hope it will give you the chance to become more efficient in your profession and help lead you to a better life.

Takashi Yasuda

Part 1

What Is Marketing?

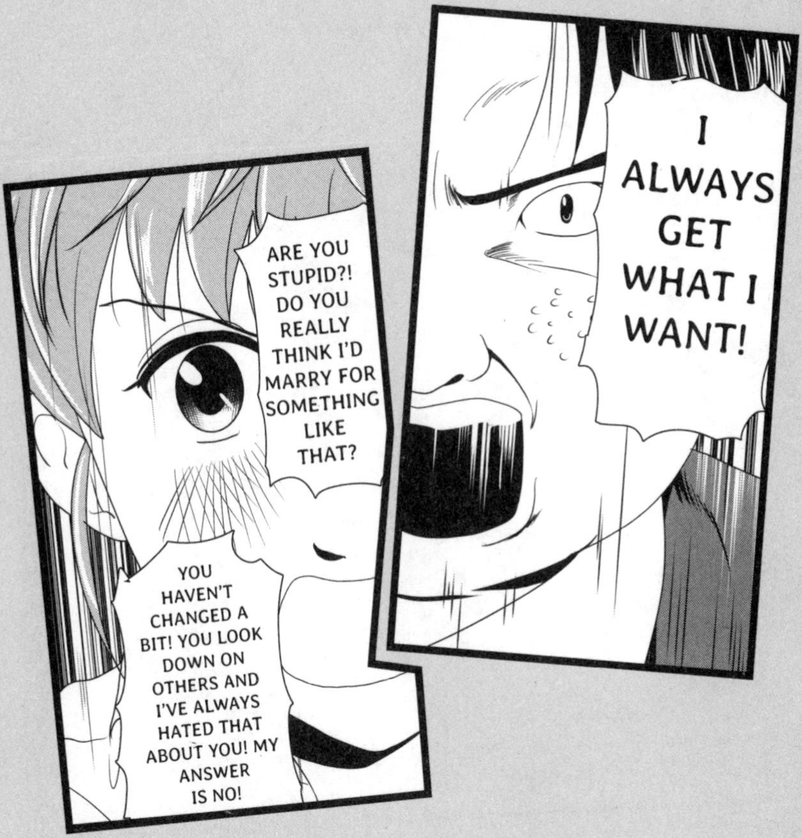
I ALWAYS GET WHAT I WANT!
ARE YOU STUPID?! DO YOU REALLY THINK I'D MARRY FOR SOMETHING LIKE THAT?
YOU HAVEN'T CHANGED A BIT! YOU LOOK DOWN ON OTHERS AND I'VE ALWAYS HATED THAT ABOUT YOU! MY ANSWER IS NO!

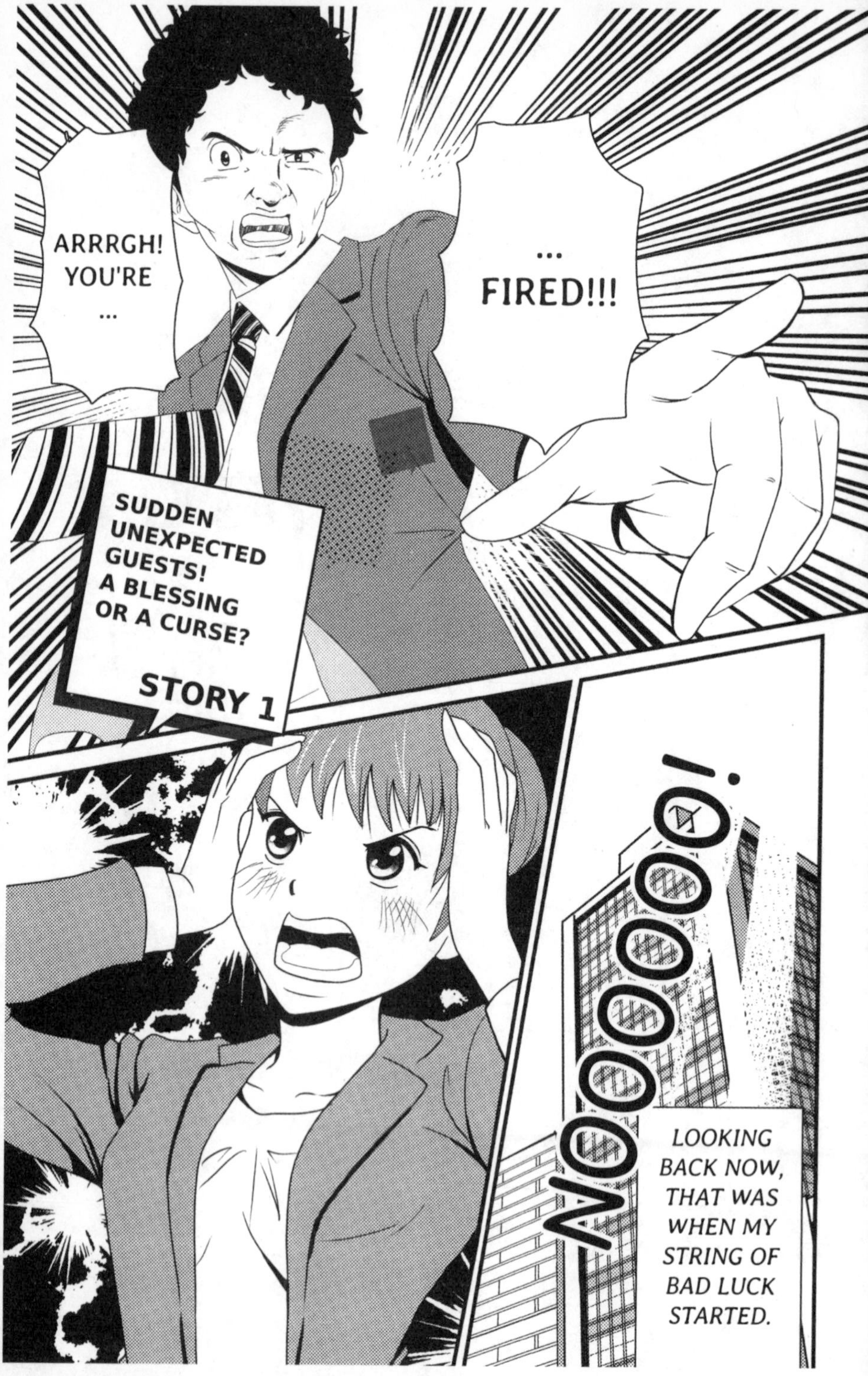
ARRRGH! YOU'RE ...
... FIRED!!!
SUDDEN UNEXPECTED GUESTS! A BLESSING OR A CURSE?
STORY 1
NOOOOOO!
LOOKING BACK NOW, THAT WAS WHEN MY STRING OF BAD LUCK STARTED.

WAAAH!

I THINK I'VE BEEN CURSED BY THE GOD OF MISFORTUNE.

NOTHING'S GOING RIGHT IN MY LIFE RIGHT NOW.

D-DON'T WORRY TOO MUCH, MARIMO! YOU KNOW OUR COMPANY HASN'T BEEN DOING WELL LATELY, RIGHT?

I BET THE CHIEF'S UNDER FIRE FROM THE HIGHER-UPS, SO HE'S PROBABLY IRRITATED.

WHY DO YOU THINK MY PROPOSAL GOT REJECTED?

I MADE SURE TO INCLUDE ALL THE SELLING POINTS.

I'M SURE THE CHIEF IS NOT GONNA FIRE YOU. OH, I KNOW! LET'S GO OUT FOR DRINKS LATER!

I'M GOOD. I'LL JUST ASK MY BOYFRIEND TO COMFORT ME.

15

Y-YOU'RE GONNA LOSE YOUR FRIENDS LIKE THAT.

WH-WHAT?

I...

...I'M BREAKING UP WITH YOU.

WHAT?! WHY?!

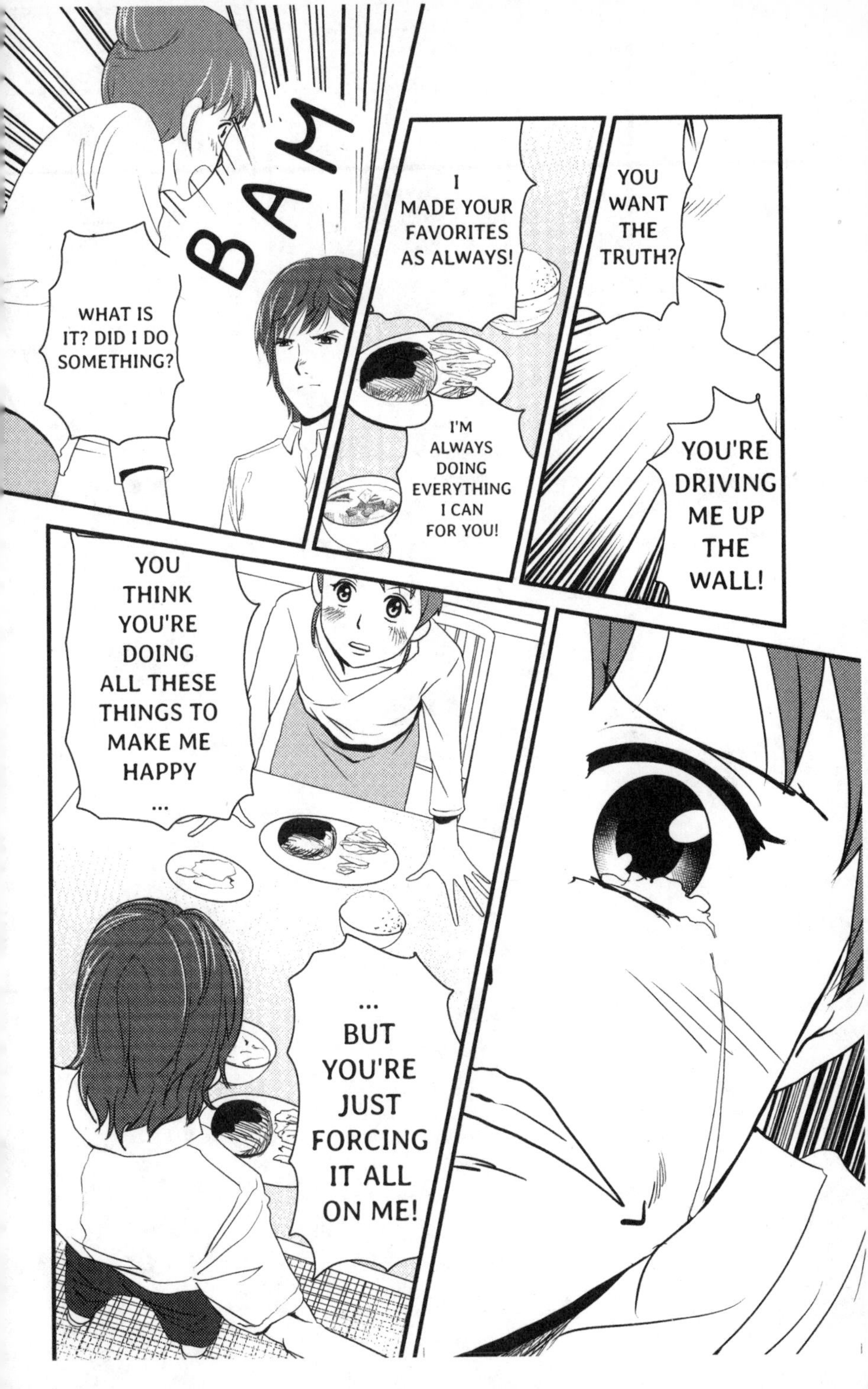
WHAT IS IT? DID I DO SOMETHING?
BAM
I MADE YOUR FAVORITES AS ALWAYS!
I'M ALWAYS DOING EVERYTHING I CAN FOR YOU!
YOU WANT THE TRUTH?
YOU'RE DRIVING ME UP THE WALL!
YOU THINK YOU'RE DOING ALL THESE THINGS TO MAKE ME HAPPY ...
... BUT YOU'RE JUST FORCING IT ALL ON ME!

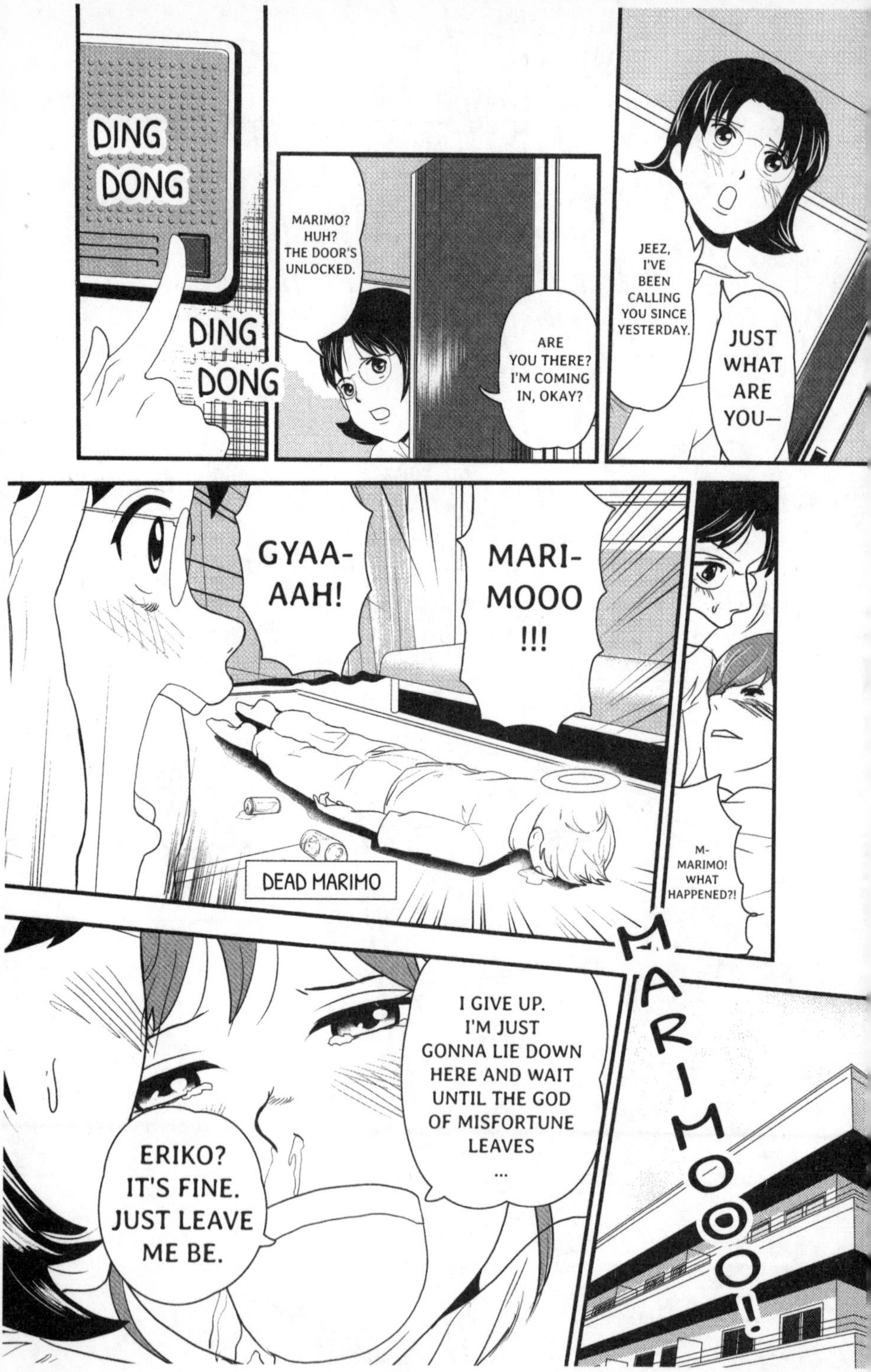
DING DONG
DING DONG
MARIMO? HUH? THE DOOR'S UNLOCKED.
ARE YOU THERE? I'M COMING IN, OKAY?
JEEZ, I'VE BEEN CALLING YOU SINCE YESTERDAY.
JUST WHAT ARE YOU—
GYAA-AAH!
MARI-MOOO!!!
DEAD MARIMO
M-MARIMO! WHAT HAPPENED?!
ERIKO? IT'S FINE. JUST LEAVE ME BE.
I GIVE UP. I'M JUST GONNA LIE DOWN HERE AND WAIT UNTIL THE GOD OF MISFORTUNE LEAVES...
MARIMOOO!

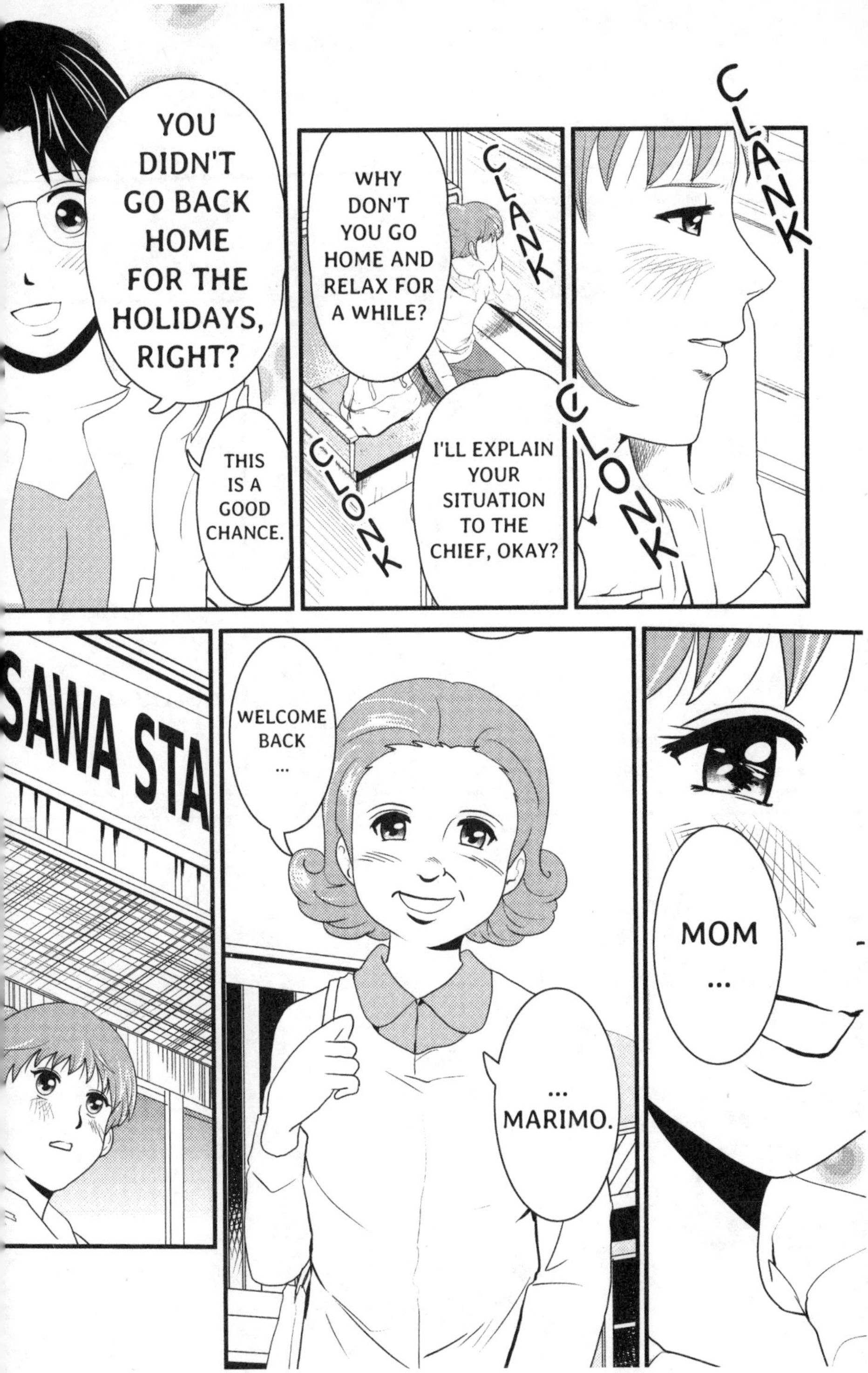

YOU DIDN'T GO BACK HOME FOR THE HOLIDAYS, RIGHT?
THIS IS A GOOD CHANCE.
WHY DON'T YOU GO HOME AND RELAX FOR A WHILE?
CLANK
CLONK
I'LL EXPLAIN YOUR SITUATION TO THE CHIEF, OKAY?
CLANK
CLONK
SAWA STA
WELCOME BACK ...
... MARIMO.
MOM ...

YOU LOOK LIKE YOU'VE LOST SOME WEIGHT, MARIMO.

REALLY? I DON'T THINK SO.

ARE YOU OKAY? HAVE YOU BEEN EATING WELL?

I'M GLAD I CAME BACK HOME. I FEEL SO CALM HERE.

OH, THE BOOK-STORE OVER THERE'S NOW A MANGA CAFE.

I GUESS WE CAN ONLY COUNT ON FAMILY IN THE END.

I'M PRETTY SURE...

Delicacy Tamaya

... THE GOD OF MISFORTUNE WON'T FOLLOW ME ALL THE WAY TO HOKKAIDO.

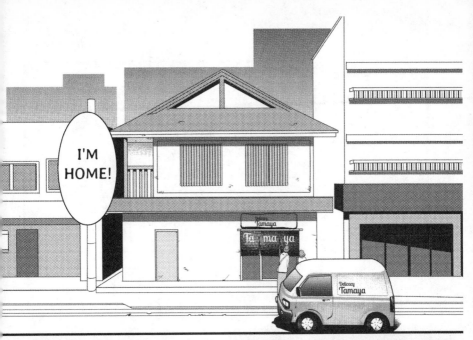

I'M HOME!

OUR FAMILY RUNS A MANJU BUN SHOP. THE BUSINESS HAS A LONG HISTORY DATING BACK 120 YEARS TO THE MEIJI ERA.

OUR LONGTIME SPECIALTY IS THE "MARIMO MANJU," A DELICIOUS SWEET BUN NAMED AFTER ME. IT'S WHAT MOST OF OUR REGULAR CUSTOMERS KEEP COMING BACK FOR.

HEY.

IT'S BEEN A LONG TIME SINCE YOU CAME BACK, BUT YOUR FATHER IS COLD AS USUAL.

HAVE YOU EATEN?

I ALREADY ATE ON THE PLANE.

WHY DON'T YOU GO AND TAKE A BATH THEN?

AHH! HOME SWEET HOME AT LAST! MY ROOM HASN'T CHANGED.

I GUESS TAKING A PAID VACATION WAS THE RIGHT CHOICE.

IT'S BEEN A WHILE. I SHOULD HELP MY PARENTS OUT TOMORROW.

ARE WE PICKING HER?

HMM, I DON'T KNOW.

SEEMS LIKE SHE'S RUNNING LOW ON LUCK.

LET'S WATCH HER A BIT MORE.

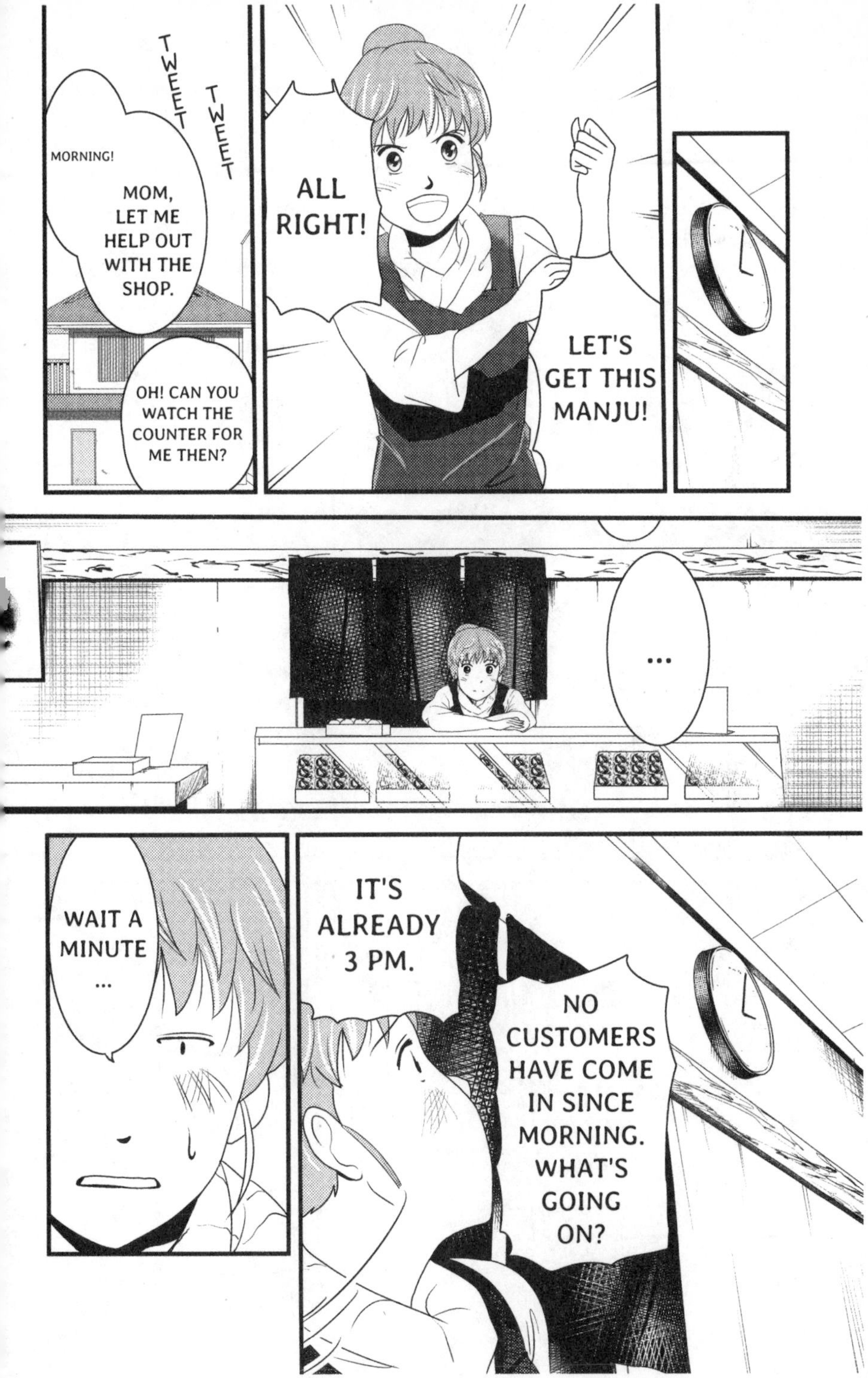
TWEET TWEET
MORNING!
MOM, LET ME HELP OUT WITH THE SHOP.
OH! CAN YOU WATCH THE COUNTER FOR ME THEN?
ALL RIGHT!
LET'S GET THIS MANJU!
...
WAIT A MINUTE ...
IT'S ALREADY 3 PM.
NO CUSTOMERS HAVE COME IN SINCE MORNING. WHAT'S GOING ON?

DAD!

B A M

SHUT UP! OUR REGULARS ARE STILL COMING IN AS USUAL.

THAT'S ALL WE NEED!

JUST OUR REGULARS? SINCE WHEN HAVE THINGS BEEN LIKE THIS?

CAN YOU REALLY KEEP RUNNING THIS SHOP?

TO TELL YOU THE TRUTH, IT'S BEEN LIKE THIS THE WHOLE YEAR.

WAIT. WHAT IS THIS?

NO WAY MY BAD LUCK CHASED ME ALL THE WAY HERE!

DOES THIS MEAN THE GOD OF MISFORTUNE IS STILL FOLLOWING ME?

VROOM

SCREECH

SLIDE

A CUSTOMER!

HEY THERE.

HUH?! YOU'RE NARUO KIZA!

THE STUCK-UP, ARROGANT GUY ...

SORRY.

WHAT?! THAT CAN'T BE TRUE!

... WHO KEPT ASKING ME OUT IN SCHOOL NO MATTER HOW MANY TIMES I REJECTED YOU!

LONG TIME NO SEE, MARIMO. I HEARD YOU WERE BACK SO I DECIDED TO PAY YOU A VISIT.

YOU'VE GOT ZERO CUSTOMERS COMING IN, HUH?

THIS PLACE IS EVEN EMPTIER THAN THE LAST TIME I WAS HERE.

120 YEARS OF HISTORY.

AT THIS RATE THOUGH, YOU MIGHT HAVE TO CLOSE UP THE SHOP SOON, HUH?

IT'S NONE OF YOUR BUSINESS. WHY ARE YOU HERE?

I'LL GET RIGHT TO THE POINT THEN.

I CAN HELP YOU SAVE THIS PLACE ...

... BUT IN EXCHANGE, YOU HAVE TO MARRY ME.

HUH?! EXCUSE ME, WHAT?

I'M SURE YOU ALREADY KNOW, BUT MY FAMILY OWNS A LARGE BAKERY BUSINESS HERE.

IT'LL BE A CINCH FOR ME TO SAVE THIS PUNY SHOP. I'VE ALREADY TALKED TO YOUR PARENTS ABOUT THIS.

TRUTH IS, KIZA BAKERY HAS BEEN OFFERING ...

... TO TAKE OVER OUR SHOP FOR MONTHS.

THE DEAL IS THAT WE'LL BECOME THEIR SUBSIDIARY AND THEY'LL HELP US REVIVE OUR SHOP.

BAH! I ALREADY SAID NO! OUR CUSTOMERS ARE DIFFERENT FROM BIG BUSINESSES LIKE YOURS!

BUT THE DEAL IS THAT YOU'LL MARRY ME IN EXCHANGE.

WHY IS THAT THE DEAL ANYWAY ?!

YOU WERE THE FIRST GIRL I EVER DEEMED WORTHY OF ME AND YOU REJECTED ME!

I BET PEOPLE WERE GOSSIPING OVER HOW I GOT DUMPED! YOU DON'T KNOW THE PAIN I WENT THROUGH!

27

I ALWAYS GET WHAT I WANT!

ARE YOU STUPID?! DO YOU REALLY THINK I'D MARRY FOR SOMETHING LIKE THAT?

YOU HAVEN'T CHANGED ONE BIT! YOU LOOK DOWN ON OTHERS AND I'VE ALWAYS HATED YOU FOR THAT! MY ANSWER IS NO!

WHAT?! YOU'RE REJECTING MY OFFER?

D- DO YOU THINK YOU HAVE THE CHOICE RIGHT NOW?!

MY ANSWER IS NO AND THAT'S FINAL! DO YOU EVEN HEAR YOURSELF?

MY LUCK HAS BEEN AWFUL LATELY, BUT IT'S STILL ...

... BETTER THAN MARRYING YOU!

WHAT?!

ARGH! WELL, WHATEVER. THERE'S NO WAY FOR YOUR LITTLE SHOP TO RECOVER ANYWAY.

I'M SURE YOU'LL COME BEGGING ME TO MARRY YOU IN NO TIME.

WHEN YOU DO, I THINK I'LL HAVE YOU KNEELING AND BOWING BEFORE ME AS YOU BEG.

IN YOUR DREAMS!

GET OUT! TAKE YOUR DELUSIONS ELSEWHERE!

GET THE DISINFECTANT.

SERIOUSLY!

WHAT'S GOING ON HERE?!

DON'T BE STUPID!

STOP DILLY-DALLYING AND GO BACK TO TOKYO! YOU WORRY 'BOUT YOUR OWN JOB!

I DO AGREE WITH YOUR FATHER, THOUGH.

WE CAN'T POSSIBLY AGREE TO MARRY YOU AWAY LIKE THAT. THERE'S NO NEED TO WORRY.

I THINK I REALLY DID GET CURSED.

WHAT DO I DO TO MAKE IT GO AWAY?

I JUST CAN'T EVEN CATCH A BREAK.

...

HA-AAH.

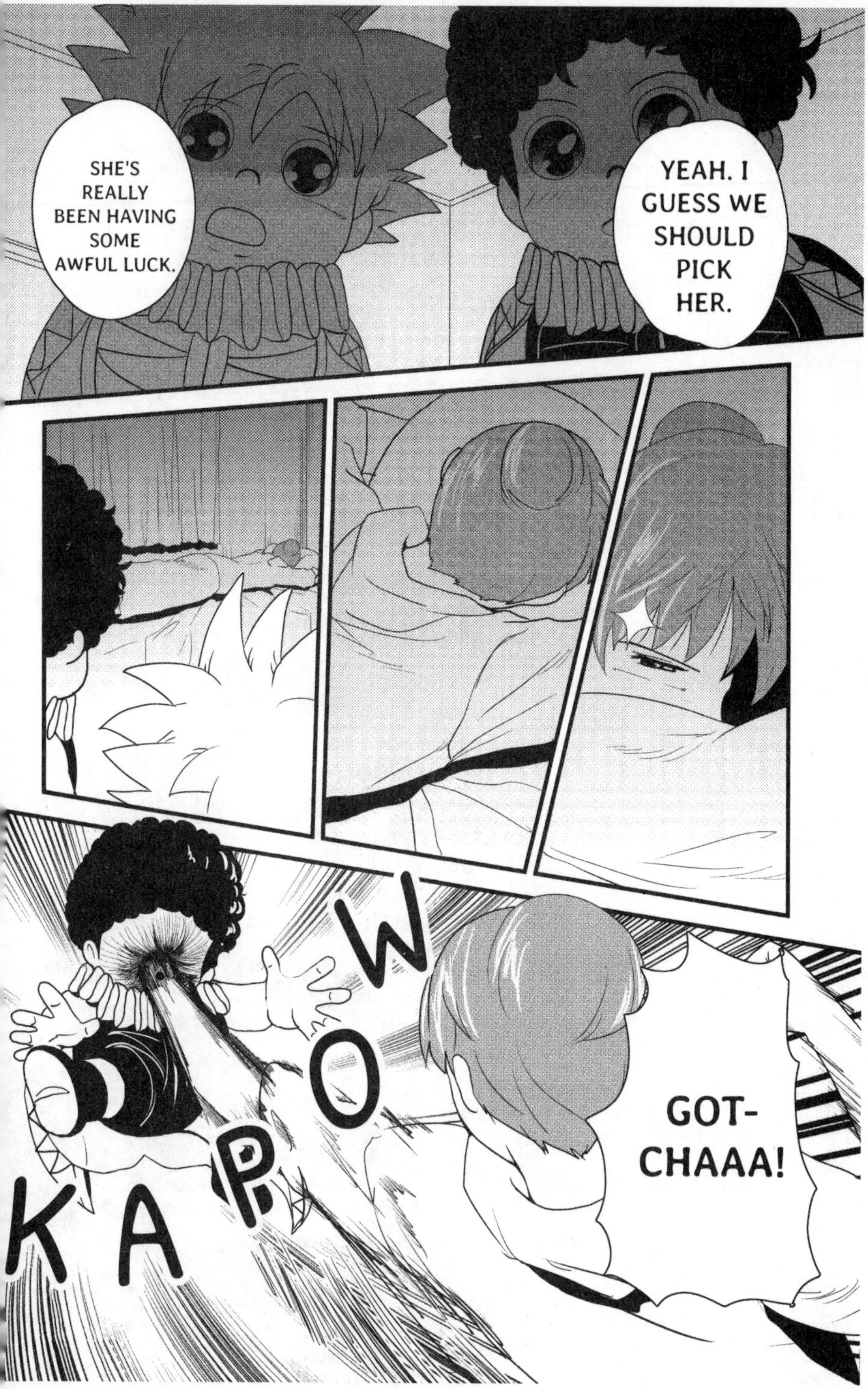
SHE'S REALLY BEEN HAVING SOME AWFUL LUCK.
YEAH. I GUESS WE SHOULD PICK HER.
KAPOW
GOT-CHAAA!

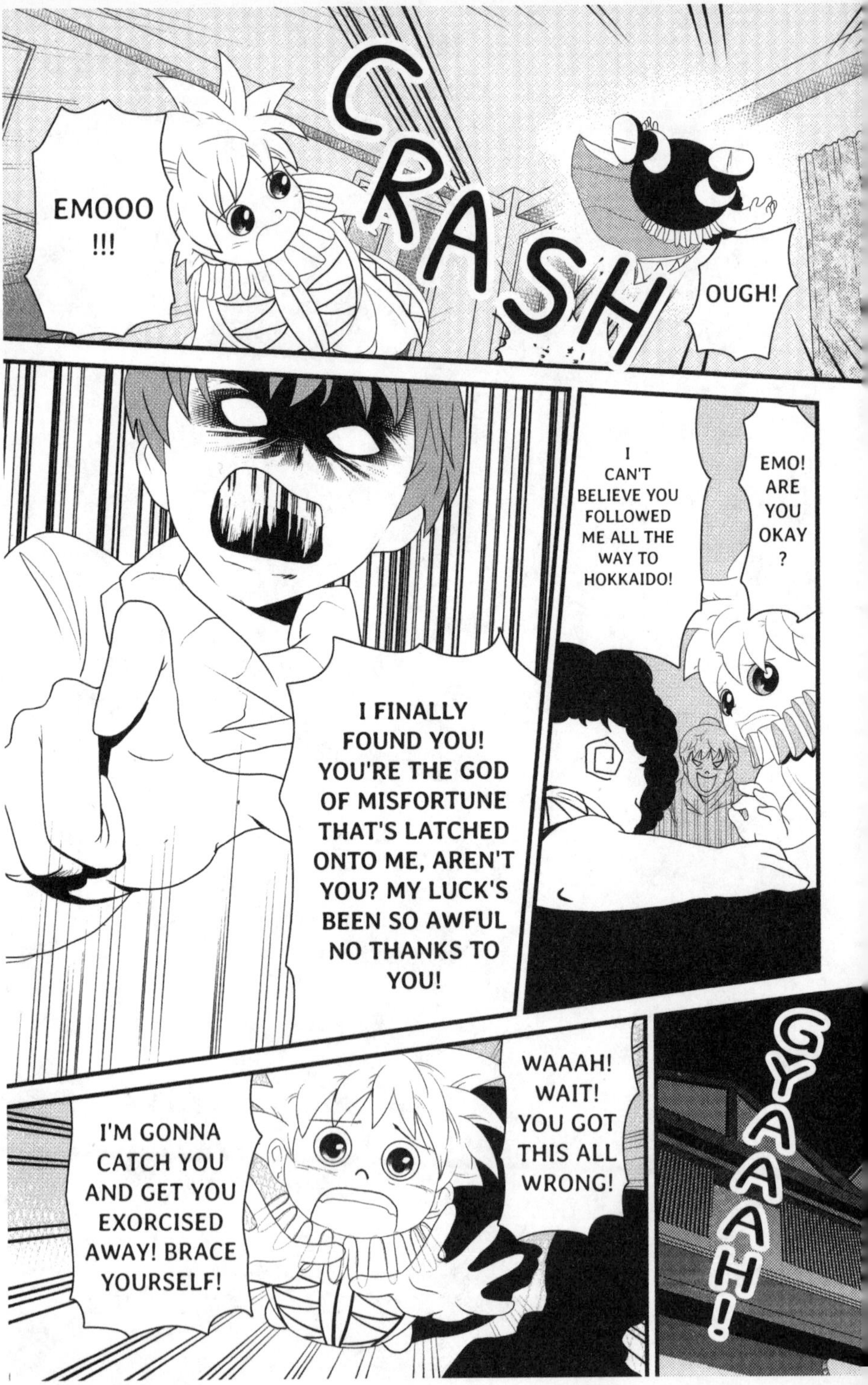
EMOOO !!!
CRASH
OUGH!
EMO! ARE YOU OKAY ?
I CAN'T BELIEVE YOU FOLLOWED ME ALL THE WAY TO HOKKAIDO!
I FINALLY FOUND YOU! YOU'RE THE GOD OF MISFORTUNE THAT'S LATCHED ONTO ME, AREN'T YOU? MY LUCK'S BEEN SO AWFUL NO THANKS TO YOU!
GYAAAAH!
WAAAH! WAIT! YOU GOT THIS ALL WRONG!
I'M GONNA CATCH YOU AND GET YOU EXORCISED AWAY! BRACE YOURSELF!

I'M LOGI!

AND I'M EMO!

WE'RE EMISSARIES FROM THE MARKETING CIRCLE OF HEAVEN!

MARKETING CIRCLE?

MARKETING EMISSARIES? WHAT?

YES! FOR CERTAIN REASONS, WE WERE SENT DOWN HERE FROM HEAVEN.

TO BE ALLOWED BACK, WE NEED TO SAVE SOMEONE'S LIFE WITH THE POWER OF MARKETING.

WE'VE BEEN LOOKING FOR A HUMAN TO HELP OUT.

THEN WE FOUND YOU! WITH HOW TERRIBLE YOUR LUCK HAS BEEN, YOU DEFINITELY NEED OUR HELP!

OKAY! NO NEED TO RUB IT IN!

ALSO, I'M NOT SOLD ON YOUR STORY YET.

BESIDES, WE JUST MET. WHAT DO YOU EVEN KNOW ABOUT MY PROBLEMS?

WELL, WE KNOW SOMEONE YOU HATE IS FORCING YOU TO MARRY HIM TO SAVE YOUR FAMILY BUSINESS.

YOU SAW THAT?

YOU'RE FAILING AT WORK AND YOUR FAMILY BUSINESS IS DYING.

AND YOU JUST GOT DUMPED BY YOUR BOYFRIEND.

TH-THAT'S GOT NOTHING TO DO WITH THIS!

THAT'S NOT NECESSARILY TRUE. HOW ABOUT A TEST, THEN?

DO YOU HAVE A TOWEL?

WILL THIS DO?

WE HAD TO WALK SOME DUSTY ROADS TO GET HERE.

WE WANT A TOWEL SO WE CAN WIPE OUR FACES.

HOWEVER, YOU'VE GOT ONLY ONE TOWEL.

BETWEEN THE TWO OF US, CAN YOU GUESS WHO REALLY WANTS THE TOWEL?

...

IT'S YOU, RIGHT?

WHY DO YOU THINK THAT?

CAUSE HIS FACE IS ALL DIRTY!

IS THAT REALLY HOW IT IS?

HUH? WHAT DO YOU MEAN?

WE DID BOTH WALK THE DUSTY ROAD ...

... BUT WE BOTH CAN'T SEE OUR OWN FACES RIGHT NOW.

I'D SEE LOGI'S CLEAN FACE ...

... AND THINK THAT MY FACE MUST BE CLEAN TOO.

ON THE OTHER HAND, I'D SEE ...

... EMO'S FACE AND I'D THINK I'M DIRTY TOO.

THAT MEANS THAT RIGHT NOW, THE ONE WHO REALLY WANTS THAT TOWEL ...

... IS ME.

YOU GOT IT WRONG.

!

I GET IT NOW!

JUST NOW, YOU JUDGED WHO TO SELL THAT TOWEL TO BASED ON OUR LOOKS AND YOUR OWN ASSUMPTIONS.

BUT, YOU DIDN'T STOP TO CONSIDER OUR THOUGHTS AND FEELINGS TO TELL WHAT WE REALLY WANT.

THIS IS TRUE FOR EVERY-THING.

IT APPLIES TO YOUR WORK AND TO YOUR BOYFRIEND TOO. YOU THOUGHT YOU WERE DOING THINGS FOR HIM, BUT YOU DIDN'T STOP TO CONSIDER WHETHER HE REALLY WANTED THOSE THINGS OR NOT.

WHAT?

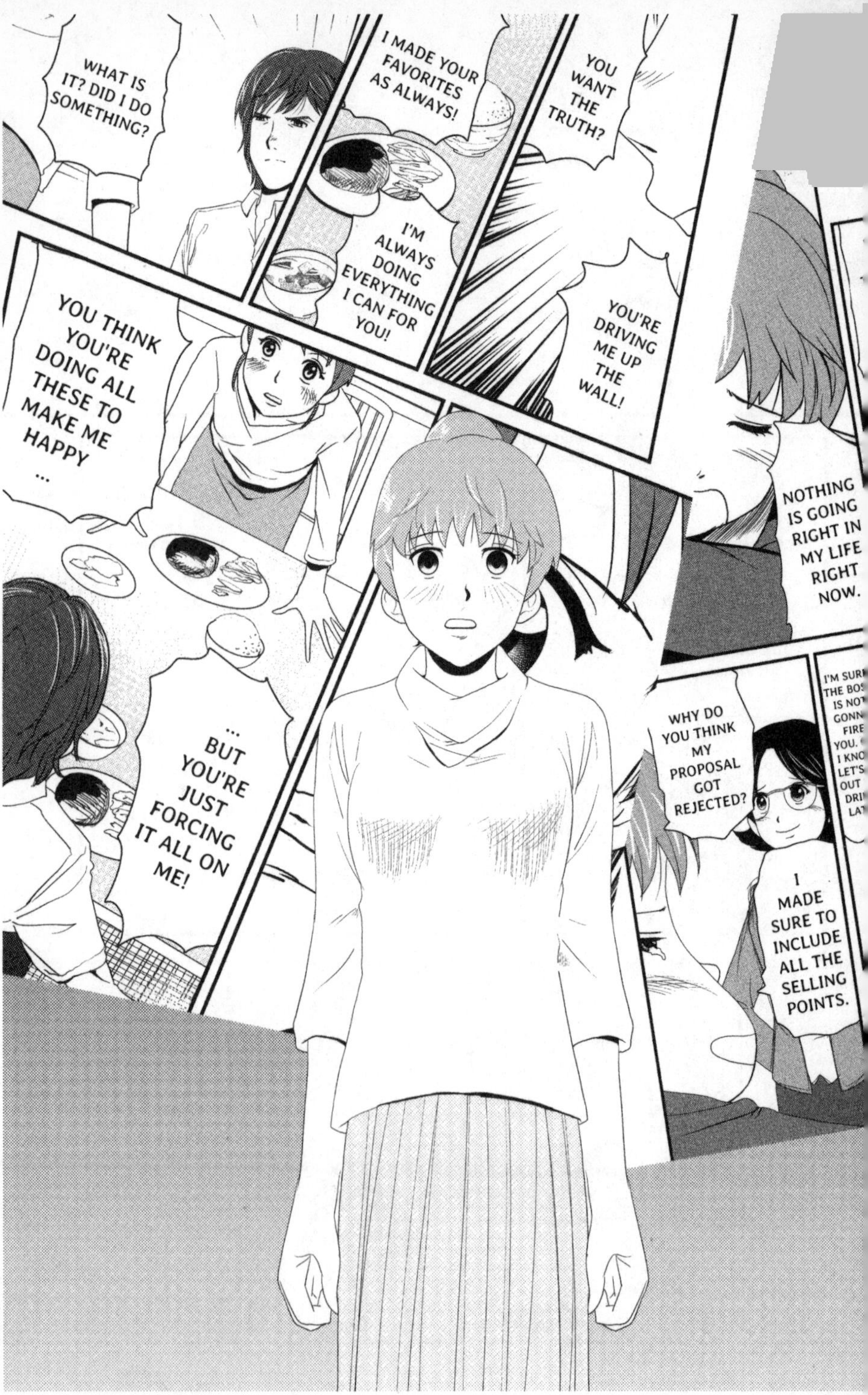
NOTHING IS GOING RIGHT IN MY LIFE RIGHT NOW.
I MADE SURE TO INCLUDE ALL THE SELLING POINTS.
WHY DO YOU THINK MY PROPOSAL GOT REJECTED?
YOU WANT THE TRUTH?
YOU'RE DRIVING ME UP THE WALL!
I MADE YOUR FAVORITES AS ALWAYS!
I'M ALWAYS DOING EVERYTHING I CAN FOR YOU!
WHAT IS IT? DID I DO SOMETHING?
YOU THINK YOU'RE DOING ALL THESE TO MAKE ME HAPPY ...
... BUT YOU'RE JUST FORCING IT ALL ON ME!

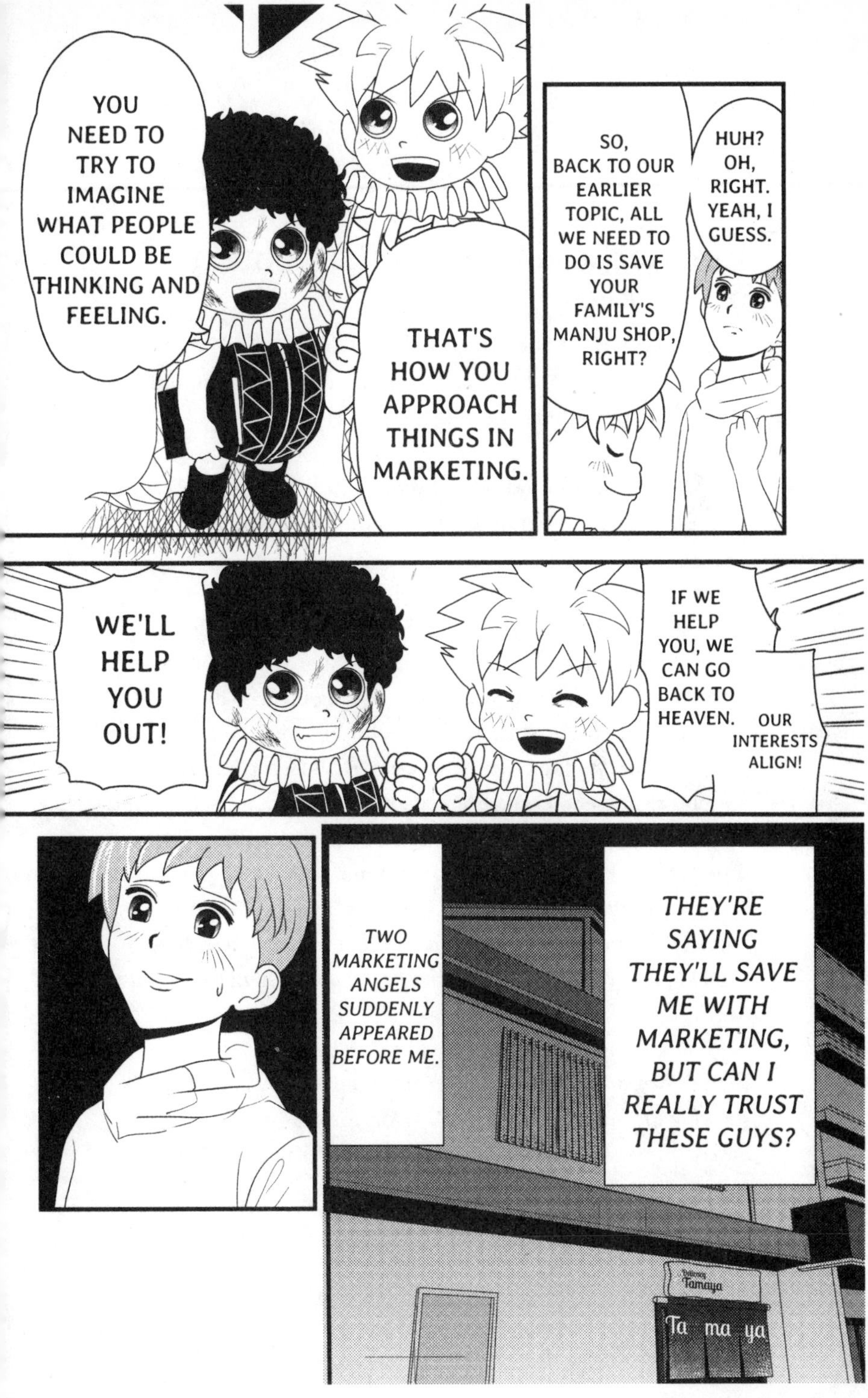
YOU NEED TO TRY TO IMAGINE WHAT PEOPLE COULD BE THINKING AND FEELING.
THAT'S HOW YOU APPROACH THINGS IN MARKETING.
SO, BACK TO OUR EARLIER TOPIC, ALL WE NEED TO DO IS SAVE YOUR FAMILY'S MANJU SHOP, RIGHT?
HUH? OH, RIGHT. YEAH, I GUESS.
WE'LL HELP YOU OUT!
IF WE HELP YOU, WE CAN GO BACK TO HEAVEN.
OUR INTERESTS ALIGN!
TWO MARKETING ANGELS SUDDENLY APPEARED BEFORE ME.
THEY'RE SAYING THEY'LL SAVE ME WITH MARKETING, BUT CAN I REALLY TRUST THESE GUYS?
Tamaya
Ta ma ya

Emotion and Logic in the Context of Marketing

What did you think about Emo and Logi's test for Marimo on page 35? Emo's face was dirty, while Logi's face was clean. How did you find their explanation regarding the answer?

Did you pick the Emo with his dirty face just like Marimo? Or did you pick the clean Logi for the reason Emo and Logi explained?

I usually ask questions similar to this in the seminars I conduct. Interestingly, people's answers often vary according to their professions. People who have jobs related to marketing, people who work in sales and management, and people who have a natural affinity for the ideas of marketing all tend to pick Logi with his clean face. On the other hand, people who work on product development, people who do regular office work, and people who have little experience in marketing all tend to pick Emo with his dirty face. I use this question in my seminars to let the participants experience what it really means to think about the customer's feelings. After they've made their choice, I ask them how they would approach the customer they chose to get them to pay for the towel.

In the story, after Emo and Logi's question, we get a flashback showing Marimo and her mistakes. Marimo has made plans based only on what she wants and has been unable to convey her good intentions. I believe that most of us have experienced making similar mistakes in the past. If Marimo learns the basics of marketing, she can avoid making these kinds of mistakes in the future.

Marketing is a communication method and tool that you can use to propose products and services that people can buy and be satisfied with. Marketing enables you to achieve excellent results by combining emotion and logic. The ability to imagine and understand your customer's emotions or mindset is very important. It is also important to use logic to come up with strategies and tactics that will lead your customers to buy what you are selling. In Part 1, we will be introducing the basic concepts you will need to study marketing.

What You Call Your Buyers Depends on the Situation

To understand marketing, you will need to know the roles related to it. To understand how products and services move from manufacturer to seller and then to buyer, let us first look at a simple everyday shopping scene.

In the simplest version, we can boil down the roles involved in marketing to two: the buyer and the seller. If we want a bit more detail, a few more characters and entities will have to make their appearance.

A manufacturer makes the product. The product is then brought into the market by wholesalers and retailers. Once circulated in the market, the consumer is able to purchase it.

In a manufacturing environment, some people plan what product to make, some develop the product, and some handle the actual production of the product. For the product to reach the buyer through the retailer, there is a supplier who buys the product from the manufacturer and a salesperson who's in charge of selling the product. There's also an advertising and promotion department responsible for letting buyers know about the product.

Finally, a consumer will buy the product from the retailer. In the world of marketing, there are many terms used for *buyer*, depending on the situation and your relationship with them. For example, if you use *buyer* as an umbrella term, the primary image given is of someone who buys the product regardless of whether they've ever bought the same product before or not. In any case, it indicates someone who buys a product.

Applying marketing ideas with this in mind directs the focus of sales promotion toward the idea of buying itself, making it difficult to consider the possibility that maybe the buyer doesn't know about the existence of the product yet. Maybe it's better to get them more interested in the product first to help them understand what they are buying.

To avoid this risk, some department stores and sellers of general products choose to think of their stores not as selling spaces but as shopping spaces. This kind of mentality helps them to always consider things from a buyer's perspective.

You will find other terms used to refer to buyers on page 44.

Different Terms for Different Buyers

Clients	Buyers who have already bought and used your product or service before
Consumers	People who may or may not have already purchased your product or service before
Customers	Anyone who buys your product or service
Potential Clients	People who live in the area covered by the company's promotions who are likely to buy the company's product
The Public	People who live in the area covered by the company's promotions, including people who will likely never buy the company's products

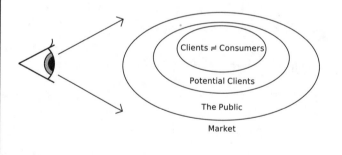

Clients ⇄ Consumers

Potential Clients

The Public

Market

The Three Points of View in Marketing

We talked about changing the term used to refer to the buyer depending on your situation, but it is also necessary to be able to change what point of view you observe your buyer from. You can take any of three points of view: (1) the point of view of the seller, (2) the point of view of the buyer, and (3) the point of view of an observer.

For example, in the exchange between Marimo and Emo and Logi (page 35), Marimo is tasked with thinking about whom to give the towel to. At this point, she is thinking from the point of view of the seller. When Marimo hears and understands their explanation, she is thinking from the point of view of both Emo and Logi (page 37). This means she is now thinking from the point of view of the buyer. As readers of this story, you observed the interaction between those three characters while thinking about what you might do in their situation. Looking at the situation from the outside like that is an example of thinking from the point of view of an observer.

When you're thinking about how to sell your product or service, it's important to look at things not only from the point of view of the buyer and seller, but also from the point of view of a third party who isn't involved in the transaction.

The Three Points of View in Marketing

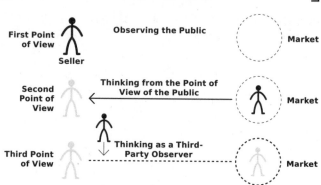

First Point of View — **Seller** — **Observing the Public** — **Market**

Second Point of View — **Thinking from the Point of View of the Public** — **Market**

Third Point of View — **Thinking as a Third-Party Observer** — **Market**

Perception from the Three Points of View

Point of View	Thought Process	What You Can Gain
First Point of View	You stay as yourself. You hear things with your own ears and see things with your own eyes.	You can gain some useful information about your own opinions and choices. If you only sway with the opinions of everyone around you, you will lose the ability to assert yourself and you will be unable to express your opinions to others. If you can't think from this point of view, you will be unable to gather essential information that others can't provide, like information about your own wants and desires.
Second Point of View	You imagine yourself as someone else. You listen as if with their ears and see things through their eyes.	You can gain more information like how your actions affect others. You will also be able to understand where another person is coming from.
Third Point of View	You push your imagination further. You try to break free from yourself to stand on a point somewhere in between yourself and others.	You can gain valuable information on the exchanges you have with others. From this standpoint, you won't get easily misled by conflicts and misunderstandings. Here, you can observe your relationships with other people and assess the effects of your actions more objectively than from any other position.

From the first point of view, you will be able to think about and organize what kind of product you really want to make or what kind of service you really want to offer. From the second point of view, you are able to think about what kind of product or service your customer would want. By looking at the product you came up with as a seller from the point of view of the buyer, you might realize that there's a big gap between what the seller and the buyer want. This is when the observer's point of view comes in handy. As an observer, you can determine whether or not the idea you came up with as a seller is too self-serving. You can then think of ways to bridge the gap you found and come up with a plan for selling your product.

By thinking from all three points of view, you should be able to come up with a product or service that will truly satisfy your customers. You should work toward being able to freely jump between the three points of view, putting them in practice as needed in your business endeavors.

If you find yourself stuck while working on a proposal, you can try going out for a walk and watching people. You can try watching the exchange between a shop clerk and a customer. Now that you've learned about these three points of view, you will find that it's easier to get hints on how to proceed with your planning. You'll probably find that you notice more things even when you're just shopping on your day off. The ability to think from different points of view is a truly valuable skill to have.

What Is Marketing?

If this is the first-ever book you've picked up on marketing, you might be wondering, "What exactly is marketing anyway?"

If you ask an academic to define *marketing*, they may point you to the definitions created by the American or Japanese Marketing Associations (see the next page).

But if you pose this question to people who deal with marketing on a daily basis, like business people or sales people, you'll get a wide variety of answers. Some would say that it has to do with the exchange between people or with some kind of barter. Others would say that it studies how to maximize benefits for both sides, that it's the essentials of business, or that it holds the secrets to profit. With recent advancements in information technology and networking, the methods used for marketing are also changing every day.

I myself see marketing as a tool we can use for different kinds of communication. I believe it's fine for everyone to find their own definition of marketing through everyday experiences.

Definitions of Marketing

AMA (American Marketing Association, 2007)

Marketing is the activity, set of institutions, and processes for creating, communicating, delivering, and exchanging offerings that have value for customers, clients, partners, and society at large.

JMA (Japanese Marketing Association, 1990)

Marketing is the comprehensive set of activities (1) used by businesses and other such organizations (2) to see things from a global perspective (3) and gain a mutual understanding with their clients and customers (4) to create a marketplace through fair competition.

Notes:
(1) Activities pertain to those concerned with research, products, pricing, promotion, and circulation as internally/externally integrated and regulated by the organization, as well as those related to customers and the surroundings.
(2) This includes educational, medical, and administrative institutions and organizations.
(3) With an emphasis on both local and foreign society, culture, and the natural environment.
(4) This includes general consumers, trade partners, and other related institutions and individuals, as well as residents of the region concerned.

How Has the Concept of Marketing Changed over Time?

Marketing concepts have changed over time. Starting with World War II and continuing to the present day, you can see that the orientation of marketers has shifted from (1) a production orientation to (2) a product orientation, to (3) a sales orientation, to (4) a marketing orientation, and, finally, to (5) a societal orientation.

A **production orientation** was favored shortly after World War II, especially in Japan. There was a shortage of almost everything and merely manufacturing something almost guaranteed that it would sell. Companies could focus only on production and expanding the circulation of their goods in order to stay in business.

Once that era ended, a **product orientation** became more useful. Supply increased everywhere and competition was born. To win against their competitors, businesses focused on product development and differentiation.

After a while, however, the supply was already meeting the demand for most goods. It became more and more difficult to stand out through product differentiation. Companies then focused on what else they could do in order to sell their products. Thus, a **sales orientation** was born.

However, as retailers kept increasing their sales promotions, the increasing pressure caused consumers to instead resist the seller's promotions. Companies realized that it would be better to find ways to make consumers happily purchase their products instead of pushing them, and thus a **marketing orientation** arose.

Today, a **societal orientation** has become prominent in marketing circles. With this orientation, companies are concerned not only with meeting consumer demands but also with society and sustainability at large. Company profit and customer satisfaction are not sufficient goals for a company; the benefits for society as a whole must also play a role in business decisions.

The Evolution of Marketing Concepts

①	**Production Orientation**	This was the concept favored when demand exceeded supply and focused heavily on production. It was centered on how to improve production while expanding circulation.
②	**Product Orientation**	With the advent of competition, companies realized that they needed to differentiate their product through development and improvement. This concept is centered on how to differentiate products. It focuses on the development of the product itself and not on consumer needs.
③	**Sales Orientation**	As competition grew fiercer, companies focused on how to get consumers to buy their products. The concept of sales promotion was born. Here, customer needs are still neglected.
④	**Marketing Orientation**	In order to meet the company's objectives, they learned to focus on trying to understand their target market and consumer needs. By selling products that consumers want, they are able to sell products more efficiently and consumer satisfaction is met. This is a concept that focuses on developing marketing strategies and plans.
⑤	**Societal Orientation**	This is a concept that not only considers company profit and customer satisfaction, but also considers the benefits for society as a whole by dealing with production waste and other environmental problems. This concept focuses on sustainability.

The Scope of Marketing

Marketing plays an important role within an organization, with its scope expanding in recent years. It is important to understand where marketing appears within the entire management process in order to use marketing strategies most effectively.

Companies often have a management strategy that concerns itself with narrowing targets and meeting customer needs. Management strategies are developed through the analysis of internal and external environments, which includes looking at the current trends in the world and the company's current state. A general strategy, case-by-case strategies, and functional strategies are then decided based on that. A marketing strategy is an example of a functional strategy.

As marketing is treated as a functional strategy within the entire management framework, it ties in heavily with management strategy. In most cases, environmental analysis and strategy development equate to marketing strategy development itself. As such, in this book, we will be tackling strategy development as well as internal and external environmental analysis (see Part 4).

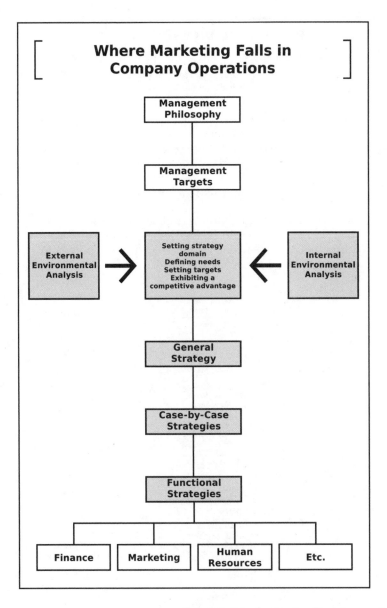

Where Marketing Falls in Company Operations

Management Philosophy

Management Targets

External Environmental Analysis → **Setting strategy domain / Defining needs / Setting targets / Exhibiting a competitive advantage** ← **Internal Environmental Analysis**

General Strategy

Case-by-Case Strategies

Functional Strategies

Finance | **Marketing** | **Human Resources** | **Etc.**

Listening to the Voice of Your Market

Using survey methods to understand the needs and wants of your consumers is called *marketing research*. Marketing research is used to develop and sell products.

The simplest marketing research method is an observational survey. For smaller companies, the person in charge of product development or members of their staff can be sent out into the world to observe people. For more thorough research or for larger companies, a research agency can be hired to conduct surveys or group interviews.

There are many methods used in marketing research. They all have their own advantages and disadvantages. The cost varies from one method to another as well. It is important to choose the one that best fits your needs.

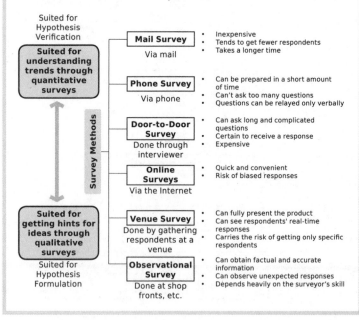

Part 2

The Pros and Cons of Viral Marketing

WILL WORD OF MOUTH REALLY BRING IN CUSTOMERS?

STORY 2

...

WHY DID YOU LET IT GET THIS BAD?

SORRY ...

NO, I'M SORRY FOR NOT KEEPING IN TOUCH.

I SHOULD'VE REALIZED IT SOONER.

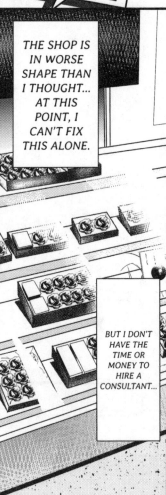

THE SHOP IS IN WORSE SHAPE THAN I THOUGHT... AT THIS POINT, I CAN'T FIX THIS ALONE.

BUT I DON'T HAVE THE TIME OR MONEY TO HIRE A CONSULTANT...

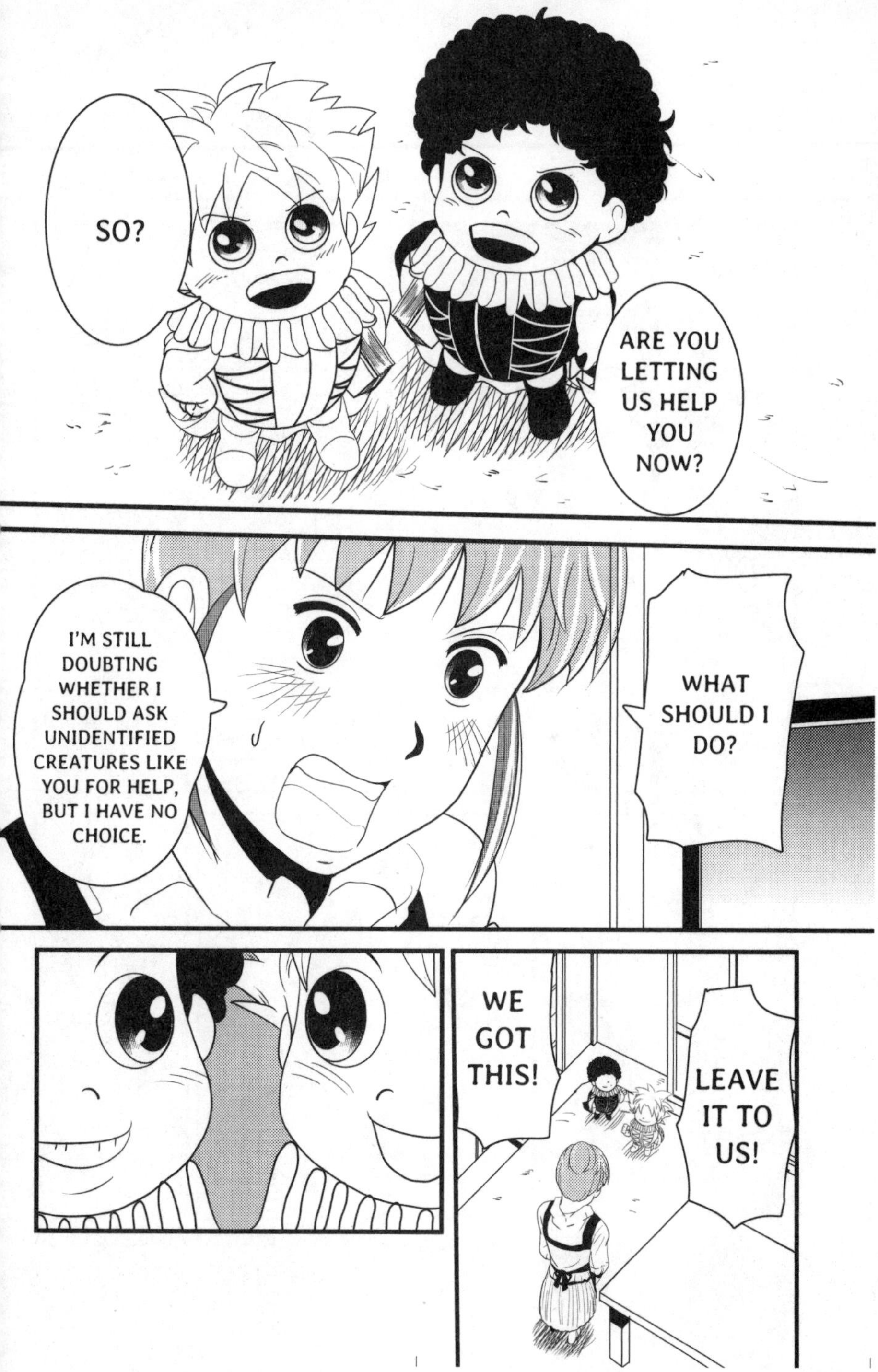
SO?
ARE YOU LETTING US HELP YOU NOW?
I'M STILL DOUBTING WHETHER I SHOULD ASK UNIDENTIFIED CREATURES LIKE YOU FOR HELP, BUT I HAVE NO CHOICE.
WHAT SHOULD I DO?
WE GOT THIS!
LEAVE IT TO US!

Delicacy Tamaya

WHAT DO I DO FIRST?

THAT'S EASY! YOU JUST GOTTA STIR THINGS UP WITH GOOD REVIEWS!

YOU CAN USE BLOGS, REVIEW SITES, AND SOCIAL MEDIA TO SPREAD GOOD REVIEWS! THAT'S SURE TO BOOST YOUR SALES FAST!

I'M AGAINST THIS CAREFREE METHOD.

FIRST, WE NEED TO STUDY HOW THEIR PRODUCTS ARE MADE. WE SHOULD CAREFULLY—

REALLY?! HOW FAST?!

OW!

BAM

YEAH. REALLY FAST!

I HAVE A JOB SO I CAN'T STAY HERE VERY LONG. I DON'T HAVE MUCH TIME!

CAN I ASK YOU FOR HELP?

HAHA HA! I'M MORE RELIABLE, RIGHT?

W-WAIT! DOING THINGS THAT WAY WILL—

CONK

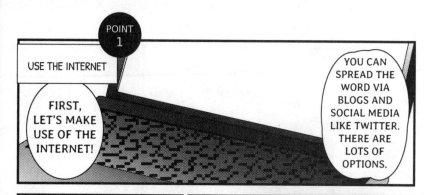

POINT 1

USE THE INTERNET

FIRST, LET'S MAKE USE OF THE INTERNET!

YOU CAN SPREAD THE WORD VIA BLOGS AND SOCIAL MEDIA LIKE TWITTER. THERE ARE LOTS OF OPTIONS.

YOU ALSO WANT PEOPLE TO GIVE YOU GOOD REVIEWS ON THE INTERNET TO RAISE PEOPLE'S OPINION OF YOUR SHOP.

YOU HAVE A POINT. I OFTEN LOOK AT REVIEWS MYSELF WHENEVER I'M LOOKING FOR SHOPS TO VISIT. WHY IS THAT?

PEOPLE ARE WARY ABOUT ADS AND PROMOTIONS ...

... BUT THEY WON'T GET SUSPICIOUS WHEN SOMEONE THEY KNOW RECOMMENDS THEM SOMETHING.

OH, I SEE!

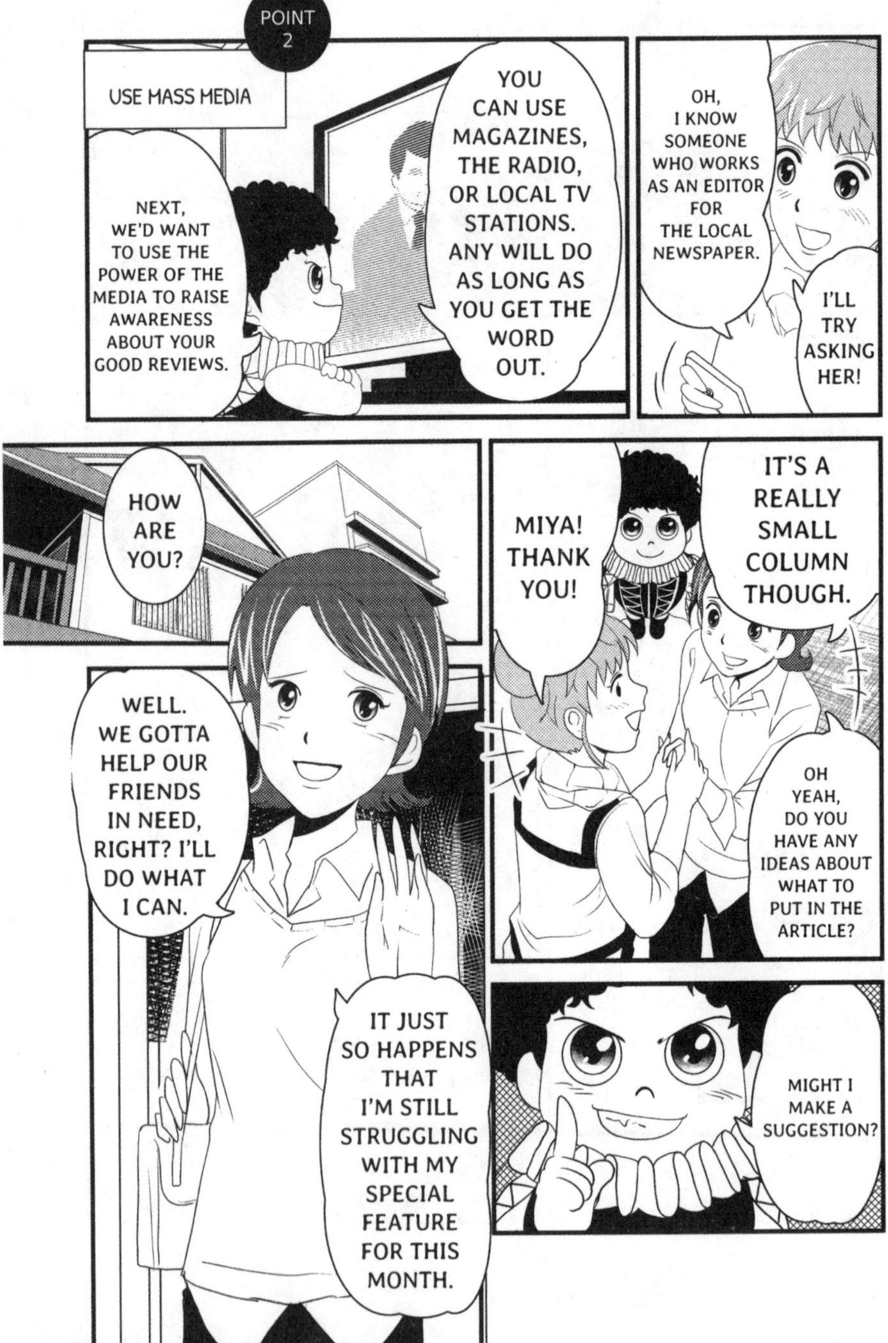
POINT 2
USE MASS MEDIA
NEXT, WE'D WANT TO USE THE POWER OF THE MEDIA TO RAISE AWARENESS ABOUT YOUR GOOD REVIEWS.
YOU CAN USE MAGAZINES, THE RADIO, OR LOCAL TV STATIONS. ANY WILL DO AS LONG AS YOU GET THE WORD OUT.
OH, I KNOW SOMEONE WHO WORKS AS AN EDITOR FOR THE LOCAL NEWSPAPER.
I'LL TRY ASKING HER!
HOW ARE YOU?
WELL. WE GOTTA HELP OUR FRIENDS IN NEED, RIGHT? I'LL DO WHAT I CAN.
IT JUST SO HAPPENS THAT I'M STILL STRUGGLING WITH MY SPECIAL FEATURE FOR THIS MONTH.
MIYA! THANK YOU!
IT'S A REALLY SMALL COLUMN THOUGH.
OH YEAH, DO YOU HAVE ANY IDEAS ABOUT WHAT TO PUT IN THE ARTICLE?
MIGHT I MAKE A SUGGESTION?

POINT 3

MAKE USE OF SCARCITY

YOU SHOULD TRY SELLING A LIMITED QUANTITY OF THE PRODUCT.

Seasonal White Marimo

IT COULD BE EVEN BETTER IF YOU MATCH THE SEASON AND CALL IT SEASONAL!

BY DOING THIS, PEOPLE WILL FEEL LIKE THEY HAVE TO BUY IT SOON OR ELSE IT'LL RUN OUT.

AH...

SLIDE

I'LL GO HOME AND WRITE ABOUT IT IMMEDIATELY! THANKS!

THAT'S RIGHT. IT'S EASIER TO TALK ABOUT LIMITED PRODUCTS.

OH, THAT'LL BE EASY TO WRITE ABOUT! LET'S GO WITH THAT!

IT GIVES PEOPLE THE CHANCE TO BRAG A BIT. AND IT'S NOT JUST FOR ARTICLES. IT CAN ALSO LEAD TO REVIEWS BY GENERAL CUSTOMERS.

61

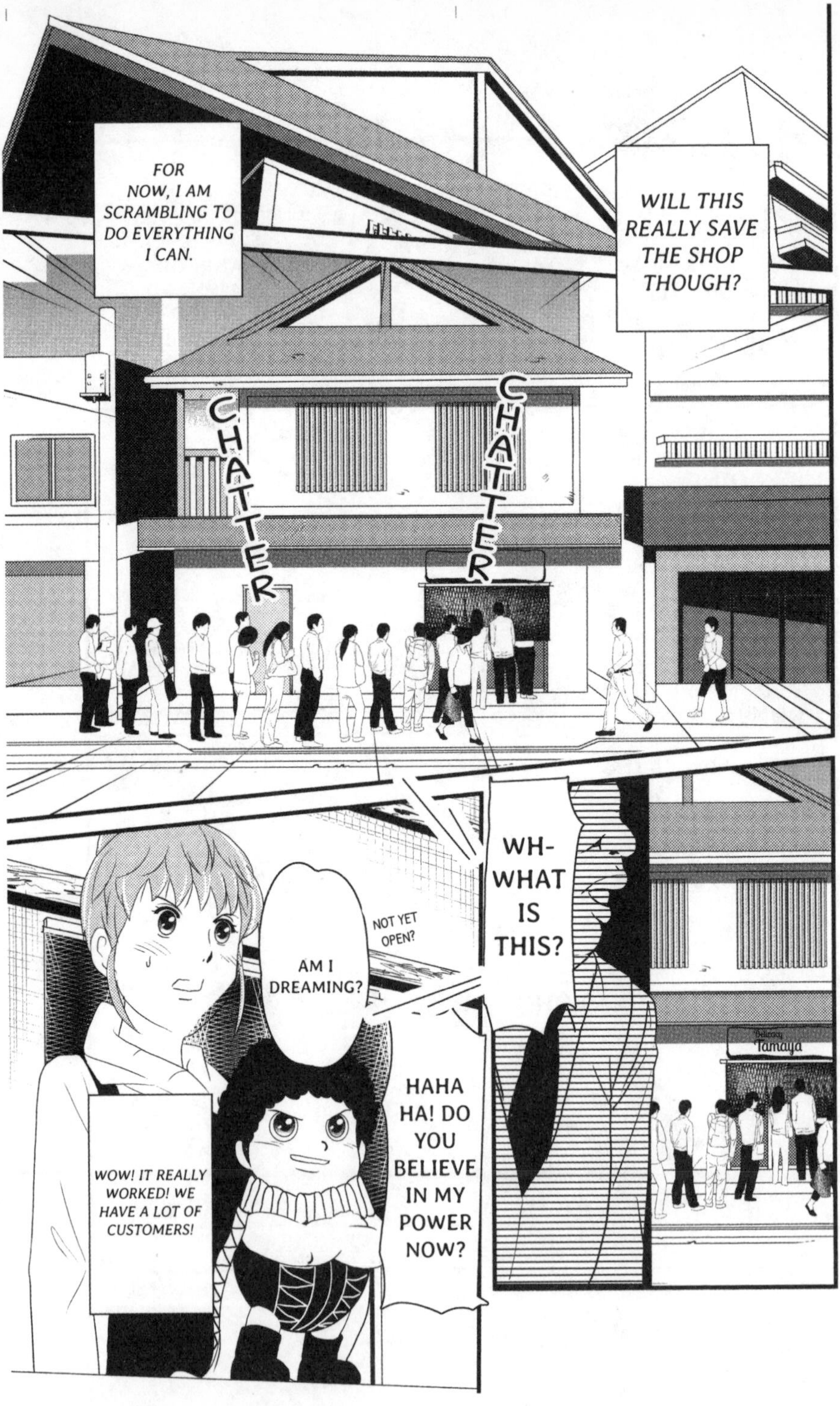
FOR NOW, I AM SCRAMBLING TO DO EVERYTHING I CAN.
WILL THIS REALLY SAVE THE SHOP THOUGH?
CHATTER
CHATTER
WH- WHAT IS THIS?
NOT YET OPEN?
AM I DREAMING?
Tamaya
HAHA HA! DO YOU BELIEVE IN MY POWER NOW?
WOW! IT REALLY WORKED! WE HAVE A LOT OF CUSTOMERS!

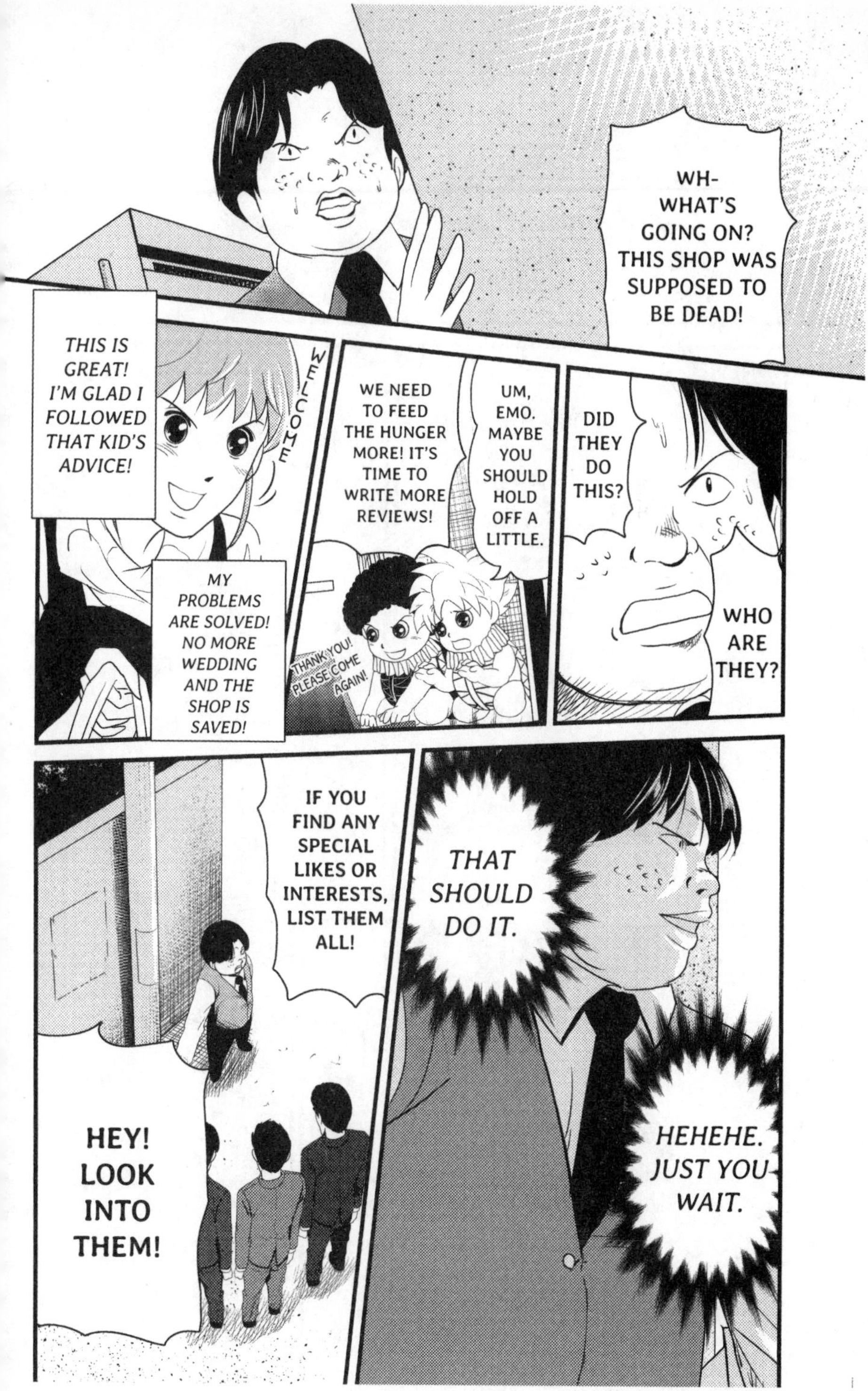
WH- WHAT'S GOING ON? THIS SHOP WAS SUPPOSED TO BE DEAD!
DID THEY DO THIS?
WHO ARE THEY?
UM, EMO. MAYBE YOU SHOULD HOLD OFF A LITTLE.
WE NEED TO FEED THE HUNGER MORE! IT'S TIME TO WRITE MORE REVIEWS!
THANK YOU! PLEASE COME AGAIN!
WELCOME
THIS IS GREAT! I'M GLAD I FOLLOWED THAT KID'S ADVICE!
MY PROBLEMS ARE SOLVED! NO MORE WEDDING AND THE SHOP IS SAVED!
THAT SHOULD DO IT.
HEHEHE. JUST YOU WAIT.
IF YOU FIND ANY SPECIAL LIKES OR INTERESTS, LIST THEM ALL!
HEY! LOOK INTO THEM!

WHEW! THIS IS SCARY!

AND I'M EXHAUSTED!

YOU CAN TAKE IT EASY NOW. LOTS OF CUSTOMERS TODAY TOO, HMM?

OH, IS THAT YOU, DEAR?

SEE, DAD? WE HAVE MORE CUSTOMERS NOW!

THIS IS THE POWER OF MARKETING! OUR SHOP IS SAVED!

...

WHAT'S UP WITH HIM?! I'M TRYING MY BEST HERE!

...

DO YOU HAVE TO BE SO COLD, DEAR? MAYBE YOU COULD PRAISE HER A LITTLE.

...

WE ACTUALLY DO HAVE A LOT MORE CUSTOMERS COMING IN.

DID YOU SEE GRANNY HIBINO COME IN RECENTLY?

HOW ABOUT GRAMPS MURAKAWA AND HIS SON? NO MATTER HOW EMPTY WE GOT, WE HAD REGULAR CUSTOMERS WHO'D COME TO BUY OUR MANJU EVERY FEW DAYS...

...BUT I HAVEN'T SEEN THEM RECENTLY.

The Influence of Word of Mouth through Viral Marketing

In the story, Emo suggests promoting their products with word-of-mouth strategies in what is known as *viral marketing*. Depending on how it's implemented, viral marketing has the potential to achieve very high promotional effects in a short amount of time. However, when this method is misused, not only will it not affect your product's sales, it may even damage the reputation of your product or company.

Compared to the more organic word of mouth born from reviews shared by actual buyers or users of a product, word of mouth that's generated by the seller tends to be quite unnatural. People who believe they are being unduly manipulated by the seller will exchange their perspective with other people over the Internet. If their perspective was based on a misunderstanding, the discussion will die there. However, if more people grow suspicious, the product may end as a one-hit wonder and in worse cases, a wave of complaints and suspicion among the company's customers may arise.

Other examples of marketing methods that tend to invite even more problems are *shock marketing* and *stealth marketing*. These types of marketing use the Internet to spread controversial content to catch people's attention. The aim is to use this attention to boost product sales. Regardless of whether they have a more direct promotional objective, strategies that introduce products or services via social media without properly explaining their objective also fall into this category. Companies risk going out of business as a result of attempting to go for quick promotional results by using blatantly deceptive methods.

What kind of promotional methods companies choose will vary and depend on their values and philosophies. Nonetheless, companies distrusted by a large number of people usually don't last very long. Marketing is, in essence, supposed to be a tool for improving the communication between the parties involved. From this perspective, fake reviews, shock marketing, and stealth marketing are strategies that should not be considered standard marketing practices and are better off not used.

As Emo explained, if reviews are written by actual users of the product or service, they will have a higher persuasive power since the information is coming from other buyers instead of the seller. As such, strategies that aim to make use of this kind of word of mouth aren't a bad idea. It's possible to trigger the spread of word of mouth by conveying details about the product. If you are able to do this, reviews published in the media will invite even more discussion. This will spread awareness about your product or service which will, in turn, increase your sales.

Devising Strategies to Boost Word of Mouth

Word of mouth can be positive, praising the quality of a product or service, or negative, pointing out flaws and complaints. People are more likely to share negative opinions about a product or service than they are positive ones. For example, when people go to a restaurant to eat, they often share negative sentiments like "Terrible. Will never visit again," "This is the worst restaurant I've ever been to," or "You're better off not eating here." On the other hand, praising something is harder as it can make people feel like they're pushing for a product or service too much. People find it harder to say, "That place is great" or "That restaurant is the best!" with conviction unless they're talking to a close friend.

Research conducted before the widespread use of the Internet and smartphones revealed that a good review from one person would reach five more people, but a bad review would reach ten. Today, with the advent of review websites, Twitter, and personal blogs, among other social media, the impact of negative reviews can be devastating to a company. Positive reviews can have the opposite effect. We are now in an era where hits are born from the words of ordinary citizens.

Given how influential word of mouth is, it's important to devise strategies that lay the groundwork to make it easier for word of mouth to generate. You should try to come up with ways to make people want to talk about your product and provide tools that they can use to spread the word.

For example, advertising companies look for things related to the product's or service's development that could become a good topic for discussion. This topic is spread through media. Other companies send sample products to influencers who can spread the word about their product. If the product is good and they are able to convey what's good about it, there is a high probability that word will spread about your product.

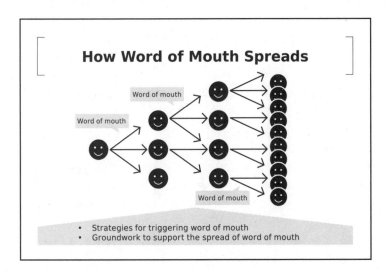

How Word of Mouth Spreads

Word of mouth

Word of mouth

Word of mouth

- Strategies for triggering word of mouth
- Groundwork to support the spread of word of mouth

Products and Services Most Affected by Word of Mouth

With the widespread use of mobile phones and the Internet, word of mouth has become even more important than before. Services, high-tech gadgets, risky products, fashion, and new products are especially strongly affected by word of mouth.

For hotels and restaurants where the quality cannot be known before a visit, people turn to the opinions of people who have visited before them. For high-tech gadgets like electrical appliances, people tend to worry about whether the new features are useful, whether the devices are user-friendly, or whether there is a problem with a new model. Consequently, people tend to ask the opinion of people who have already purchased the same model. For cosmetics and financial products, people want to avoid the risks associated with these types of purchases. For fashion products, people look at others' opinions to avoid standing out in a bad way.

For standard products that most people already know, consumers can judge the value for themselves and so word of mouth doesn't hold much influence. Nonetheless, even standard products may still be unfamiliar to some people, and positive reviews can be highly effective in drawing new customers to a business. We saw this in the manga where Tamaya's manju buns sold better with the use of viral marketing strategies.

Products Most Affected by Word of Mouth

Type of Product	Reason	Example
Services	Usually, no free trials are offered so there is no way to evaluate the quality of the service before paying for and using it.	Hotels, restaurants
High-Tech Gadgets	Technology enthusiasts aside, the average person usually finds these difficult to use and can't understand their functions and features.	Home appliances
Risky Products	Choosing the wrong product carries a risk, i.e., choosing the wrong cosmetics can lead to skin problems, and choosing the wrong financial product can lead to financial losses.	Cosmetics, financial products
Fashion	Fashion choices depend a lot on preferences, and people are concerned about being unable to keep up with changing trends.	Apparel
New Products	With new products, all buyers are first-time buyers and will be unfamiliar with them.	Entirely new products that aren't just improved models

STRATEGIES FOR SPREADING GOOD REVIEWS ARE IMPORTANT, BUT BAD REVIEWS TEND TO SPREAD MORE EASILY SO CAUTION IS ADVISED!

Hints for Boosting Word of Mouth

Several years ago in Japan, a "million-yen broom" was featured on television news programs. The broom was made from corn tassels that were very scarce and difficult to harvest. The tassels were gathered over many years to make a single broom. As a result of the media attention to the broom and its manufacture, sales of the broom increased.

This kind of fresh and interesting topic is the type that's easily picked up by the news. Even without paying for ads, you can get the media to feature your company's product. You can get more credibility, attention, and impact by having your product featured in an article than you can from running ads.

Similar stories include restaurants that serve multi-thousand-dollar desserts covered in gold, celebrities insuring their limbs for millions of dollars, and other attention-grabbing promotions. There are many stories like these and you probably have seen them quite often in periodicals and on television.

In the following chart, you'll find some angles you can explore to create this kind of word of mouth, and, in line with Emo's explanation regarding rarity, you will also find some ideas for unique added value that you can attach to your products to boost the spread of word of mouth.

Angles You Can Utilize to Trigger Word of Mouth

Angle	Example
Who	Identify well-known people who can endorse your products or services, including actors and celebrities.
When	Look for timely topics that can be easily picked up by news or weather programs. • Things that people can easily associate with a season, like daffodils and cherry blossoms • The year's firsts, like the first snow or the first day of summer
Where	Look for newsworthy topics related to a place. • Value of the place itself • The first ever in the area • Places that make people go, "Why here?"
Why	Build on product credibility by presenting reasons and bases for it. • Numbers and data • Explaining the product with actual video footage
What	Look for newsworthy topics regarding the product. • The product itself • The effectiveness of the product ingredients according to research
How	Convey information on why your methods are unique. • Never been done before (manufacturing process) • A completely new method of selling
How much	Discover surprising facts related to pricing. • A broom shop that sells a super luxury broom for a million dollars • A luxury cake that costs $10,000 a piece • An envelope for cash gifts worth a million dollars

Added Value That Can Boost Word of Mouth

Things That Can Feel Like Added Value	Example
Extras	• Additional items included with purchase • Raffles
Information Content	• Feng shui • Color schemes • Fortune-telling • Trivia
Originality/ Uniqueness	• Customizability • Categorization • Age limitation • Lifestyle
Excitement	• Prepare something consumers can be excited about • Go beyond the excitement • Include surprises with purchase
A Bargain	• The big effect of a small extra • Price determines value • Place determines value • Bundles feel like bargains • Charm pricing makes it feel cheaper • Just pricing feels like a bargain • Make things feel cheaper through the psychological wallet • Know when to use discounts (offer discounts on top brands)
Rarity	• Use the power of limited supply • Use the power of being time-limited • Share some secret information • Convey the increasing rarity of your product • Utilize scarcity to make your product more attractive

Source: The Techniques of Adding Value through Psychological Marketing by Takafumi Yamashita (Zen-nichi Publishing Co.)

Part 3

Understanding the People Who Buy Your Products

WHAT DO YOUR CUSTOMERS REALLY NEED?

STORY 3

GU-LP

GU-LP

CLONK

CLINK

THERE ARE MORE RUDE CUSTOMERS NOW.

I GUESS TAMAYA HAS REALLY CHANGED.

I FEEL LIKE I CAN'T GO IN AND BUY THEIR MANJU LIKE I ALWAYS HAVE.

THANK YOU! PLEASE COME AGAIN! OH, WELCOME.

MOM! I NEED SOME HELP HERE!

O-OH, RIGHT.

OUR REGULARS ALL STOPPED COMING RECENTLY.

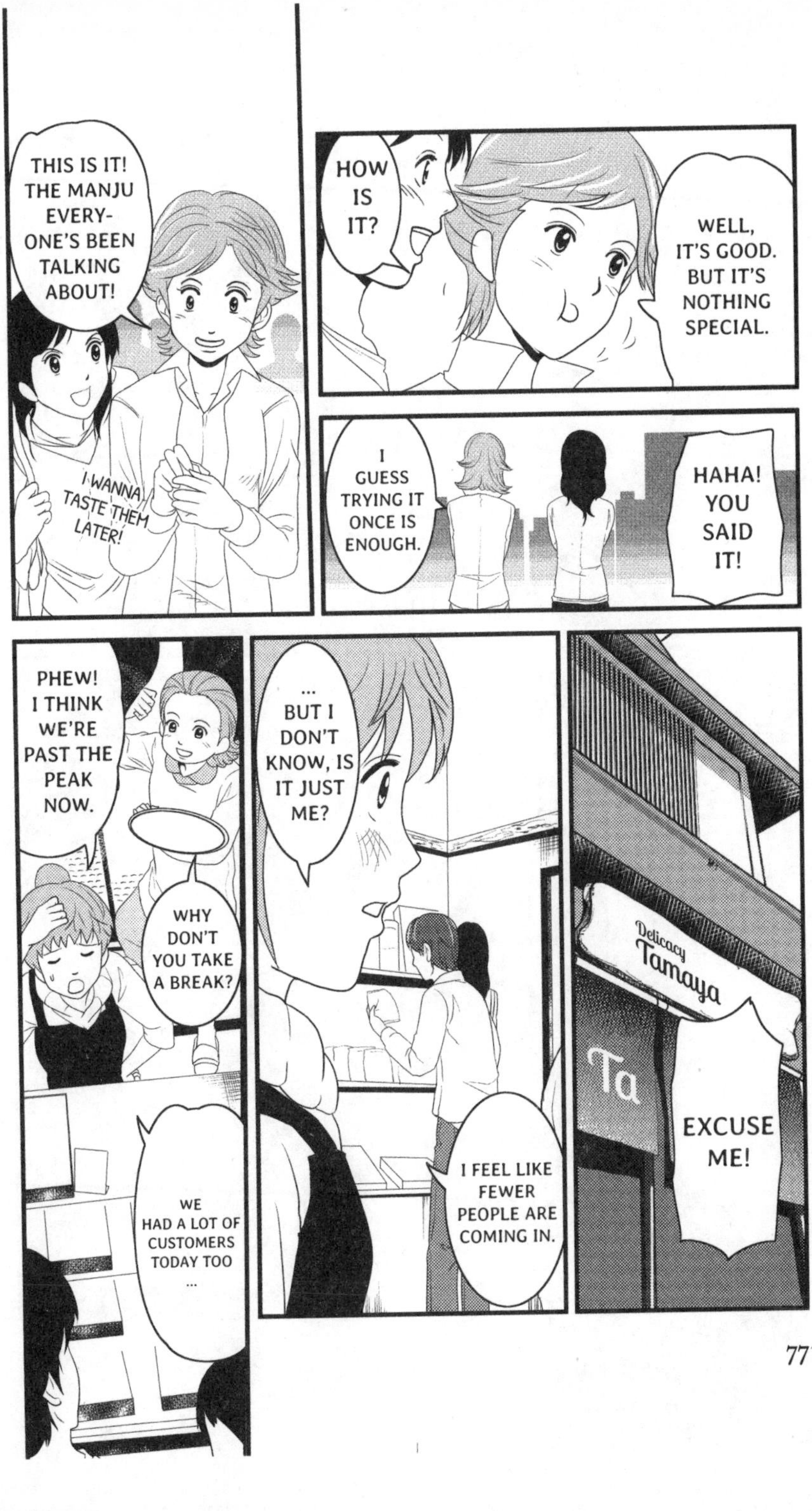
THIS IS IT! THE MANJU EVERYONE'S BEEN TALKING ABOUT!
I WANNA TASTE THEM LATER!
HOW IS IT?
WELL, IT'S GOOD. BUT IT'S NOTHING SPECIAL.
I GUESS TRYING IT ONCE IS ENOUGH.
HAHA! YOU SAID IT!
PHEW! I THINK WE'RE PAST THE PEAK NOW.
WHY DON'T YOU TAKE A BREAK?
WE HAD A LOT OF CUSTOMERS TODAY TOO ...
... BUT I DON'T KNOW, IS IT JUST ME?
I FEEL LIKE FEWER PEOPLE ARE COMING IN.
Delicacy Tamaya
Ta
EXCUSE ME!

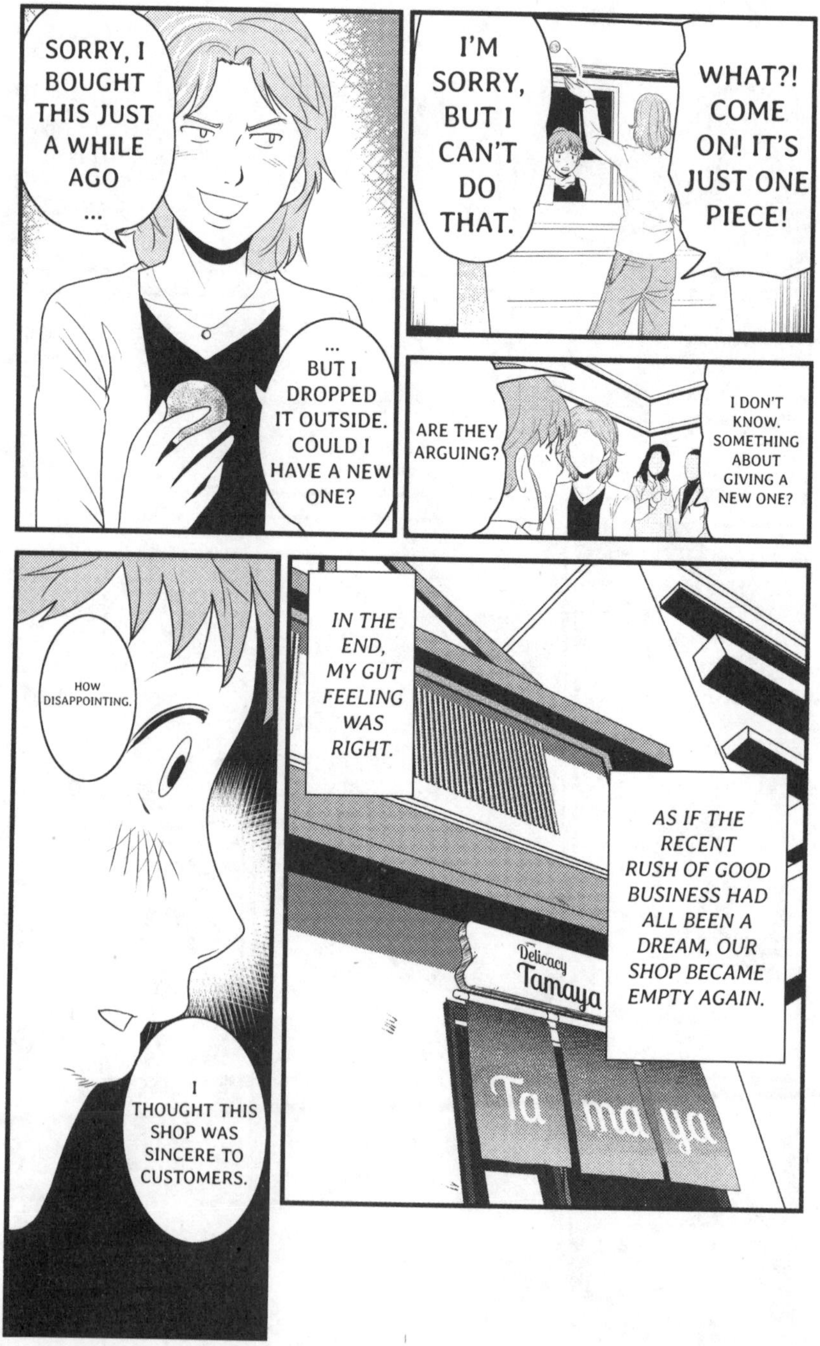
SORRY, I BOUGHT THIS JUST A WHILE AGO ...
... BUT I DROPPED IT OUTSIDE. COULD I HAVE A NEW ONE?
I'M SORRY, BUT I CAN'T DO THAT.
WHAT?! COME ON! IT'S JUST ONE PIECE!
ARE THEY ARGUING?
I DON'T KNOW. SOMETHING ABOUT GIVING A NEW ONE?
HOW DISAPPOINTING.
I THOUGHT THIS SHOP WAS SINCERE TO CUSTOMERS.
IN THE END, MY GUT FEELING WAS RIGHT.
AS IF THE RECENT RUSH OF GOOD BUSINESS HAD ALL BEEN A DREAM, OUR SHOP BECAME EMPTY AGAIN.
Delicacy Tamaya
Ta ma ya

W-WELL, I DON'T KNOW...

IT'S TRUE. SUDDENLY NO ONE'S COMING.

EMO! I DID AS YOU SAID!

BUT THE CUSTOMERS ONLY CAME ONCE!

YOU DID GET A LOT OF PEOPLE TO BUY OUR MANJU BUT ONLY...

...FOR A SHORT WHILE. OUR REGULARS STOPPED COMING TOO.

IF THIS IS THE MARKETING YOU'RE TALKING ABOUT. I'M DISAPPOINTED.

...

OH! THIS IS IT!

THIS ONE!

WE WANT ...

... THIS.

HELLO! WHERE ARE YOU GUYS FROM?

MARI-MO ...

FROM MIDORICHO! WE SAW YOUR SHOP ON TV.

WE'RE ON OUR WAY TO GRANDMA'S HOUSE, SO WE THOUGHT WE'D BRING SOME MANJU.

... DO YOU KNOW HOW YOU MANAGE TO ATTRACT THESE TWO CUTE CUSTOMERS?

KNOWING THAT CAN HELP YOU FIGURE OUT HOW TO ATTRACT MORE CUSTOMERS.

THIS IS ONE OF THE FUNDAMENTAL IDEAS USED IN MARKETING ...

AIDMA?

■ AIDMA

Attention: You caught their attention via local TV or newspapers.
Interest: You got them interested because "Grandma might like this."
Desire: Now they want your manju because they want Grandma to taste it.
Memory: They remember that a store called Tamaya sells manju.
Action: They then take action by buying your product on the way to Grandma's house.

OH, SO THAT'S HOW YOU THINK ABOUT IT!

THERE ARE TWO MORE CONCEPTS YOU SHOULD TAKE NOTE OF.

THAT'S THE IDEA OF NEEDS AND WANTS.

OH, I KNOW THAT.

IT MEANS THE KIDS HAVE THE NEEDS FOR MANJU, RIGHT? HUH? WAIT, WHAT ARE WANTS THEN?

?

WHAT'S THE DIFFERENCE BETWEEN NEEDS AND WANTS?

■ NEEDS AND WANTS

> **Needs:** Things that people feel they need
> **Wants:** Unrealized potential desires

THEY DIDN'T KNOW ABOUT YOUR MANJU BEFORE, RIGHT? DO YOU THINK THEY WANTED MANJU IN THE FIRST PLACE?

NO, I DON'T THINK SO. YOU CAN'T WANT SOMETHING YOU DON'T KNOW ABOUT.

RIGHT. WHEN THOSE KIDS DIDN'T KNOW ABOUT YOUR MANJU YET ...

... THEY WOULD'VE BOUGHT OTHER DELICACIES INSTEAD. THAT'S THE WANTS STAGE.

NOW THAT THEY KNOW ABOUT YOUR MANJU, THEY WANT TO BUY IT. THAT'S THE NEEDS STAGE.

THAT MEANS YOUR MANJU TURNED FROM AN UNREALIZED WANT INTO A KNOWN NEED.

YOU NEED TO DO SOMETHING MORE THAN JUST SELL A LOT OF MANJU.

THE FIRST IS ...

... TO SELL YOUR MANJU TO THOSE WHO ALREADY KNOW THEY WANT IT.

THE OTHER IS TO LET THE PEOPLE WHO WOULD POTENTIALLY WANT YOUR MANJU KNOW ABOUT ITS EXISTENCE.

YOU NEED TO GUIDE YOUR POTENTIAL CUSTOMERS INTO BUYING YOUR PRODUCT. THAT'S THE BASIC IDEA OF MARKETING.

SO ALL THIS TIME, I'VE BEEN TRYING TO ATTRACT CUSTOMERS WITHOUT EVEN KNOWING THESE BASICS.

I GUESS THEY'RE GETTING ALONG.

DOES THAT MEAN MY METHODS WERE WRONG?

BUT THEY HAPPILY LISTENED TO ME WHEN THINGS WERE GOING WELL.

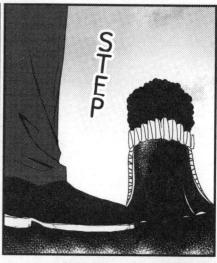

STEP

YOUR METHODS AREN'T WRONG AT ALL.

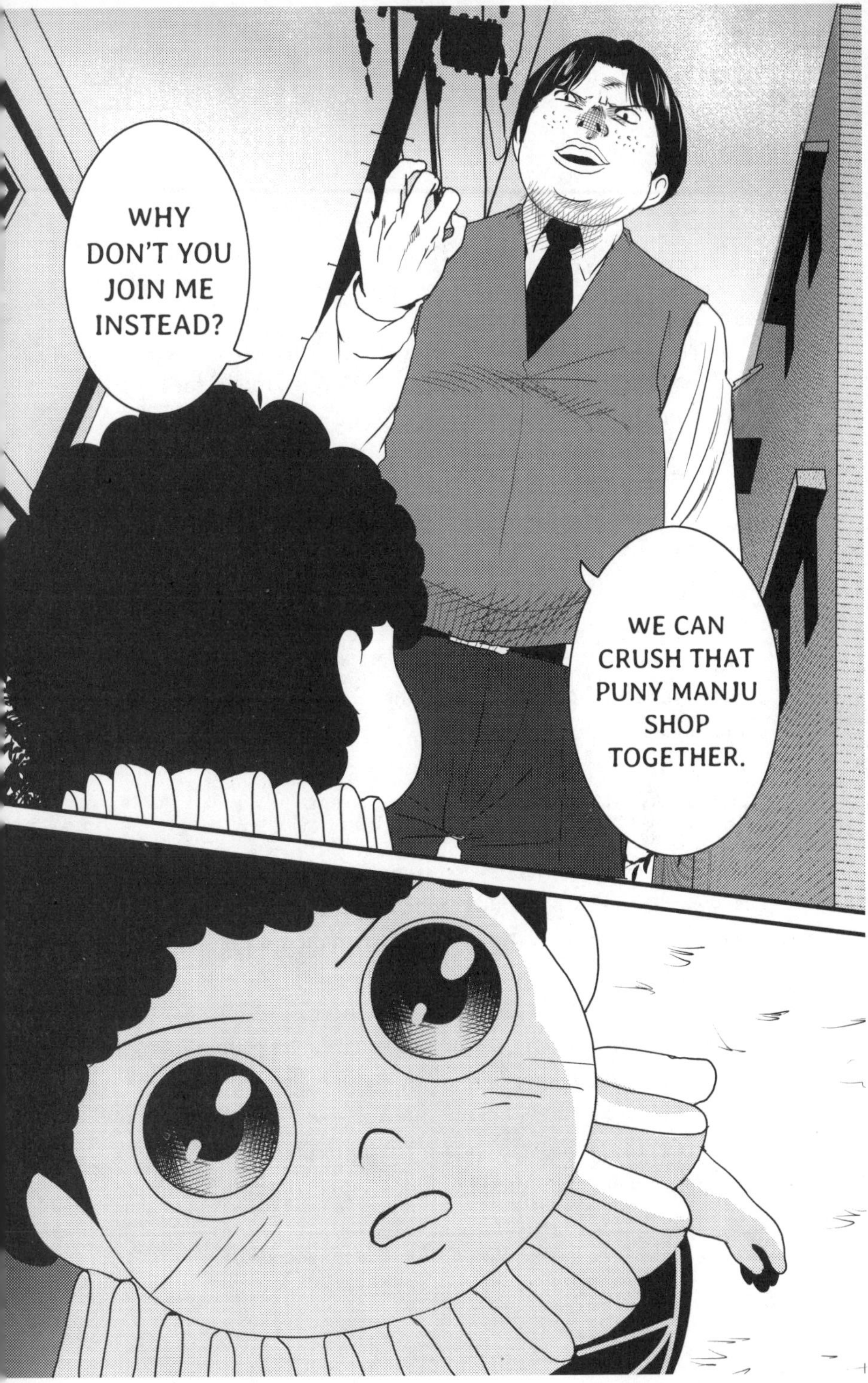
WHY DON'T YOU JOIN ME INSTEAD?
WE CAN CRUSH THAT PUNY MANJU SHOP TOGETHER.

The AIDMA Model of Consumer Behavior

On page 80, two siblings come in to purchase manju and Logi starts explaining the AIDMA model. **AIDMA** is a model for explaining the changes that occur in people's mental states as they decide to buy a product. The model divides the process that a consumer goes through—from noticing a product until they actually purchase it—into five steps.

First, (1) a person notices a product via ads or promotions (Attention) which gets them (2) interested in the product (Interest). After that, they will end up (3) wanting the product (Desire) and eventually (4) remember it (Memory). Finally, (5) they will look for the product and buy it (Action). This shows the changes in consumers' actions and the thoughts that consumers have as they go about purchasing a product. AIDMA is an acronym for these steps.

Of course, not all purchases go through exactly these five steps. However, knowing about this model makes it easier to think of promotional strategies that cater to each of these steps.

In Tamaya's case, Emo proposed spreading the word through social media and making use of local media to let people know about their product. Not only are they able to let people know about the product itself, but they are also able to tell people about the product's features and appeal. This leads people to become interested in and want their product in one fell swoop. For TV ads, repetition steers people to remember a product, which can then influence people's actions.

By being aware of what step a consumer is currently on based on the AIDMA model, you can devise plans and strategies that can steer them toward the next step. In doing so, you can increase sales while satisfying consumers.

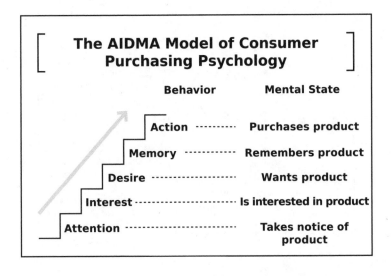

The AIDMA Model of Consumer Purchasing Psychology

Behavior	Mental State
Action	Purchases product
Memory	Remembers product
Desire	Wants product
Interest	Is interested in product
Attention	Takes notice of product

The AIDMA Model as Applied to Purchasing a Smartphone

		Mental State	**Example (Smartphone)**
Step 1	Attention	Takes notice of product	You read about a new smartphone model on the Internet.
Step 2	Interest	Is interested in product	You learn that it has functions your current model doesn't have and think it would be nice to have.
Step 3	Desire	Wants product	You look at online reviews and ratings for that model and you decide that you want it.
Step 4	Memory	Remembers product	You make a mental note to go to a physical store on the weekend to try it out yourself.
Step 5	Action	Takes action to purchase the product	It's the weekend and you go to the physical store to try it out. You're satisfied and you now try to negotiate the best deal for it.

THE MODEL PRESENTS THE STEPS THAT A POTENTIAL CUSTOMER GOES THROUGH.

Models That Explain Purchasing Behavior

THERE ARE DIFFERENT MODELS FOR EXPLAINING CONSUMER BEHAVIOR. THE AMTUL MODEL IS USEFUL FOR REPEAT PURCHASES, WHILE AIDAS IS MORE USEFUL FOR EXPLAINING ONLINE SHOPPING. IT MIGHT BE GOOD TO USE DIFFERENT MODELS DEPENDING ON WHAT KIND OF PURCHASE YOU'RE LOOKING AT.

	Main Scope	Notes
AIDA Model	Covers traditional purchasing behavior from advertising to product circulation in stores	The base of the AIDMA model; not widely used in Japan
AIDMA Model	Covers traditional purchasing behavior from advertising to product circulation in stores	The traditional and standard model
AMTUL Model	Covers purchasing behavior for products that tend to be purchased repeatedly	Provides a value index for the customer's behavior for each step
AIDAS Model	Covers all purchasing behavior driven by information gathering and sharing via the Internet	Explains traditional online purchasing behavior
AIDEES Model	Covers all purchasing behavior driven by information gathering and brand building via the Internet	A model focused on brand building through word of mouth
Kotler's Consumer Buying Decision Process Model	Covers purchasing behavior based on typical data processing	Includes post-purchase assessment

2

What Is the Kotler Consumer Buying Decision Process Model?

Philip Kotler, the foremost American scholar of marketing, developed a decision-making model that is used today by marketers around the world. His **Consumer Buying Decision Process Model** looks at the purchasing process from a different angle than the AIDMA model. Here, the five-step process begins with a consumer realizing that they want something and ends with them making that purchase and evaluating their purchase.

The process starts with (1) problem recognition in which a person realizes that they want something to satisfy a certain need. The person then (2) gathers information on products or services that would potentially satisfy this need and (3) evaluates them.

If the person decides that a different product is better or that they don't need to buy the product right now, the process will stop there. However, if they decide that there are no problems, they will (4) decide to purchase the product and (5) evaluate their purchase afterward. If they are satisfied with the purchase, they will possibly repeat this purchase or spread good reviews. On the other hand, if they aren't satisfied with the purchase, they won't repeat it and they may share bad reviews as well. This model is unique in that it includes the negative reaction that may arise from the person's dissatisfaction with the purchase.

As with AIDMA models, by understanding this model you will be able to find promotion strategies that will cater to the different stages of consumer purchase behavior more easily.

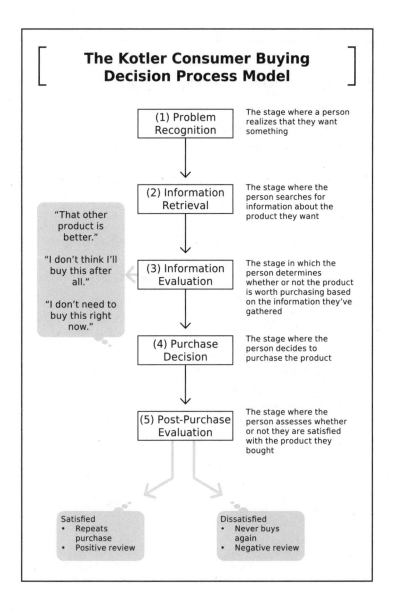

The Kotler Consumer Buying Decision Process Model

(1) Problem Recognition

The stage where a person realizes that they want something

(2) Information Retrieval

The stage where the person searches for information about the product they want

"That other product is better."

"I don't think I'll buy this after all."

"I don't need to buy this right now."

(3) Information Evaluation

The stage in which the person determines whether or not the product is worth purchasing based on the information they've gathered

(4) Purchase Decision

The stage where the person decides to purchase the product

(5) Post-Purchase Evaluation

The stage where the person assesses whether or not they are satisfied with the product they bought

Satisfied
- Repeats purchase
- Positive review

Dissatisfied
- Never buys again
- Negative review

Human Desire: Needs versus Wants

Logi explains the concept of needs and wants on page 82. There are multiple interpretations of needs and wants, and scholars and business people are divided in their opinions.

The simplest way to think about them is to take the concepts just as they are. Needs are things that you need and wants are things that you feel you want.

According to Kotler, needs are things required to survive and wants are specific things that can satisfy those needs. When needs are not satisfied, the person feels deprived.

Many who work in marketing in Japan define needs as things that consumers feel they need or want, while wants are things that consumers have yet to realize they want. For the sake of convenience, this book will adopt this interpretation to explain consumer needs and wants.

Models That Explain Purchasing Behavior

	Mental State	What Are Needs?	What Are Wants?	Example
Interpretation 1	Needs are necessary, and wants are desires.	Things that you feel you need or need to do	Things that you want or want to do	Regular vehicle inspection is a requirement if you own a car. In this case, the service becomes a need. On the other hand, even if you want a Porsche, your car doesn't need to be a Porsche. You can have other cars, so in this case, a Porsche becomes a want and not a need.
Interpretation 2	Needs are things that you really need, and wants are a means to getting those things.	Things that you feel are necessary and therefore want	Specific wants that you have in order to satisfy your needs	Sellers often confuse needs and wants. A drill manufacturer will think that their customers need a drill bit, but what the person really needs is a hole.
Interpretation 3	Needs are wants you've realized, while wants are your potential needs.	Things that you realize you want	Things that you have yet to realize you want	Before the Internet existed, there was hardly anyone who wanted a service like it. This is the "wants" state. When the Internet came into existence, people who experienced using it realized their need for such a service. It became a need that people wanted to use whether at home or outside.

Thinking with Both Consumer Needs and Wants in Mind

The needs and wants matrix on the next page is a tool that lets you visualize a person's realized needs and unrealized wants.

When a person knows about a product and they think they want it, that means that "a need exists." This is when consumers think, "Oh, I want to buy those manju for Grandma" or "I want to eat those manju." In both cases, the consumer has a specific and realized want that they have in mind. On the other hand, there are cases when a consumer doesn't want a product whether they know about it or not. That is the state when "no need exists." When a consumer thinks, "I want to buy something for someone I'm visiting" or "I want to eat something yummy," they are expressing nonspecific wants and do not yet know what product will satisfy those wants. This is the case where "a want exists." When a consumer is unaware of the product but also doesn't feel like they want anything, this is the state where "no want exists."

As Logi explained to Marimo, it is important to promote your product to the people who fall under the "a need exists" category in this matrix. But beyond that, **if you can promote your product to people with matching unrealized needs, you will be able to gain new customers and consequently increase your sales.**

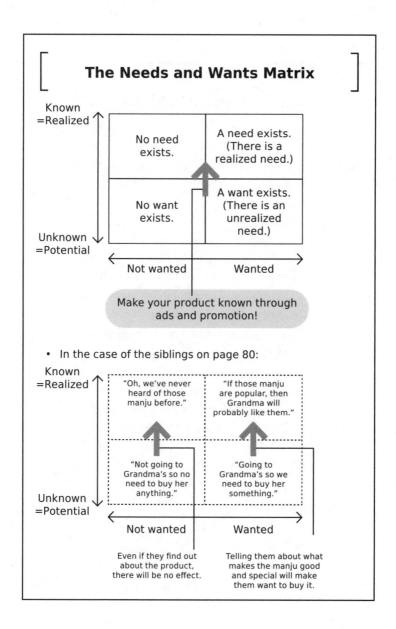

The Needs and Wants Matrix

Known
=Realized

| No need exists. | A need exists. (There is a realized need.) |
| No want exists. | A want exists. (There is an unrealized need.) |

Unknown
=Potential

Not wanted   Wanted

Make your product known through ads and promotion!

- In the case of the siblings on page 80:

Known
=Realized

| "Oh, we've never heard of those manju before." | "If those manju are popular, then Grandma will probably like them." |
| "Not going to Grandma's so no need to buy her anything." | "Going to Grandma's so we need to buy her something." |

Unknown
=Potential

Not wanted   Wanted

Even if they find out about the product, there will be no effect.

Telling them about what makes the manju good and special will make them want to buy it.

Understanding Human Needs

Besides the concept of needs and wants, another model that's useful for understanding human needs is Maslow's Hierarchy of Needs. This model organizes human needs into a five-level pyramid. Human needs move from one level to the next as the needs in the lower level get satisfied. For example, once (1) physiological needs are satisfied, (2) the need for safety is born. Once the need for safety is satisfied, humans then feel (3) the need for love and belonging, followed by (4) the need for self-esteem. The first four need levels are classified as deficiency needs, and they arise from deprivation. The highest-level need, (5) the need for self-actualization, is called a growth need. It does not arise from any sort of deficiency but is instead a need for something a person hasn't known or experienced before.

Once you know on which of the five levels your customer is currently on, you will be able to offer them the appropriate product. For example, if a customer has an unstable life and doesn't feel safe, you can offer products or services that would help solve those problems. On the other hand, you can offer customers who are already on the self-actualization level products and services that will help them improve themselves through cultural enrichment.

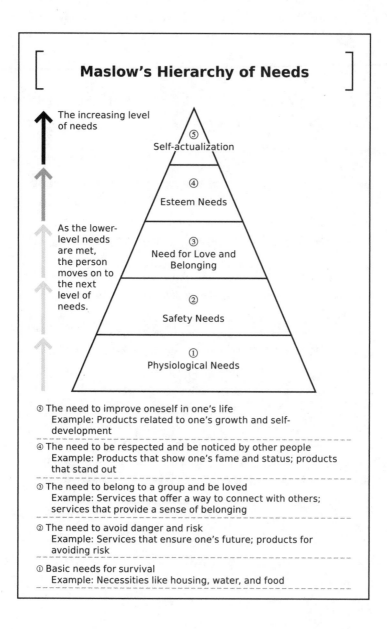

Maslow's Hierarchy of Needs

The increasing level of needs

⑤ Self-actualization

④ Esteem Needs

③ Need for Love and Belonging

② Safety Needs

① Physiological Needs

As the lower-level needs are met, the person moves on to the next level of needs.

⑤ The need to improve oneself in one's life
Example: Products related to one's growth and self-development

④ The need to be respected and be noticed by other people
Example: Products that show one's fame and status; products that stand out

③ The need to belong to a group and be loved
Example: Services that offer a way to connect with others; services that provide a sense of belonging

② The need to avoid danger and risk
Example: Services that ensure one's future; products for avoiding risk

① Basic needs for survival
Example: Necessities like housing, water, and food

Buyers Who Set the Trend and Buyers Who Follow the Trend

Knowing when a customer decides to buy a product is also important in understanding buyers. For instance, if you look at the people around you, are there people who pay attention to trends and try out anything that people seem to be talking about? What about people who only buy something once it gets good reviews? Do you see these different types of people around you?

Innovation theory can be used to explain how a product or service spreads among people. Trends begin from the innovative and progressive types of people, the *innovators*. These are enthusiastic people who show a keen interest in products and services. These types of people are intent on experiencing a product's value for themselves. The next quickest people to react are called the *early adopters*. They look at the innovators' response to the product and if they think it's good, they'll actively try to get their hands on the product. They are also sometimes called *opinion leaders*, and just as this name suggests, they tend to be the ones who introduce new products to other people. They are a group who likes to be at the forefront of new trends. If this group responds positively to your product, there is a high chance that it will sell.

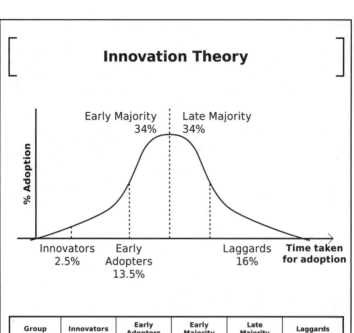

Innovation Theory

Group	Innovators	Early Adopters	Early Majority	Late Majority	Laggards
Type	Adopts new things earliest	Perceptive to trends; gathers information on new products and judges it for themselves	More cautious about new trends; careful and take time to adopt new things but are still a little earlier than most	More skeptical about new trends; wait until the majority around them has adopted a product and they've confirmed a good reception for it before adopting it themselves	The most conservative group; doesn't like change and indifferent to new products; will wait until innovations become the standard before adopting them
Also called	Progressives	Opinion Leaders	Bridge People	Followers	Conservatives
Percentage	2.5%	13.5%	34%	34%	16%

The next group to react is the *early majority*, which respond to the early adopters. The *late majority* then adopts the product once they see people around them using it.

The last group to respond to is the *laggards*. People in this group are indifferent to new products and tend to be conservative. They don't respond until most people around them are using the new product. They will then hesitantly adopt the new product once they feel cornered by the need to use it.

Part 4

Sorting out Your Company's Relationship with Your Customers

FAKE MARIMO MANJU BUNS APPEAR!

STORY 4

YOUR MANJU'S NOW IN CONVENIENCE STORES AND SUPERMARKETS, RIGHT?

HUH?

OH? I THOUGHT I SAW SOME LAST TIME. THEY LOOKED THE SAME.

IT CAME OUT OF NOWHERE.

NO WAY!

!

Authentic Marimo Manju

Authentic Marimo Manju

Authentic Marimo Manju

WH-WHAT IS THIS?

102

THE SELLER TURNED OUT TO BE THAT SNOBBISH RICH-BRAT'S KIZA BAKERY.

THAT BIG BUSINESS THAT HAS THE BIGGEST MARKET SHARE IN THE WHOLE OF HOKKAIDO IS SELLING AN IMITATION OF OUR MANJU.

DID THAT GUY JUST REALLY PULL THIS TRICK ON US?

THIS IS THAT MANJU EVERYONE'S TALKING ABOUT, RIGHT? FROM THAT OLD SHOP, TAMAYA?

BUT IT KINDA TASTES JUST LIKE ANY REGULAR MANJU, DOESN'T IT?

THIS IS BAD! WE HAVE A PROBLEM!

MARIMO, JUST CALM DOWN FOR A BIT!

CALM DOWN?! I CAN'T BE CALM ABOUT THIS!

NOW NOBODY WILL BUY OUR MANJU!

EVEN MORE UPSETTING IS THAT IT DOESN'T TASTE GOOD.

WELL, THE PACKAGING DOESN'T HAVE OUR NAME ON IT. THEY CHANGED THE NAME A BIT.

BUT NOW IT'S GONNA AFFECT OUR REPUTATION!

WE'RE UP AGAINST A BIG COMPANY! EVEN IF WE SUE, WE'LL GO BUST BEFORE THE TRIAL ENDS!

W-WAIT!

LET'S TRY LOOKING AT THIS THROUGH A MARKETING LENS.

MARIMO, YOU'VE ONLY BEEN THINKING ABOUT YOUR OWN SHOP SO FAR. WHAT ELSE SHOULD YOU CONSIDER?

YOU MEAN OUR CUSTOMERS, RIGHT?

I DO GET THAT.

WHAT ELSE?

OH!

YOU MEAN OUR NOW RIVAL COMPANY, DON'T YOU?

THAT'S RIGHT. CONSUMER ANALYSIS, COMPETITOR ANALYSIS, AND ANALYSIS OF YOUR OWN COMPANY.

THESE THREE MAKE UP WHAT WE CALL THE 3C ANALYSIS.

BUT RIGHT NOW, TAMAYA AND KIZA BAKERY ARE JUST ON A WHOLE DIFFERENT SCALE.

FOR NOW, LET'S TRY ANALYZING THIS SHOP AND ITS CUSTOMERS.

Delicacy
Tamaya

Ta ma ya

BUT KIZA BAKERY IS DOING US DIRTY! IS THAT EVEN ALLOWED?

105

THAT'S THE COPYCAT STRATEGY (ME-TOO MARKETING).

IT'S A STRATEGY USED BY BIG COMPANIES ON OTHER COMPANIES THEY SET THEIR EYES ON.

HMM? SPEAKING OF DIRTY STRATEGIES, SOMEONE COMES TO MIND ...

IT CAN'T BE, CAN IT?

LET'S THINK ABOUT THIS SHOP'S COPYCAT STRATEGY (ME-TOO MARKETING).

STILL, IT'S A REALLY DIRTY TRICK!

I'D LIKE TO SEE THE SHAMELESS FACE WHO DID THIS!

ACH-OO!

S N I F F

106

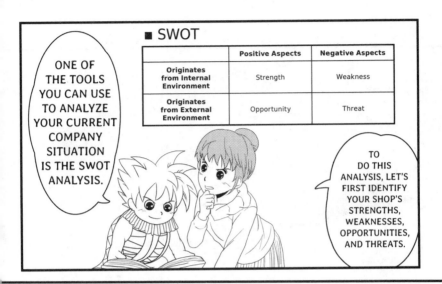

■ SWOT

	Positive Aspects	Negative Aspects
Originates from Internal Environment	Strength	Weakness
Originates from External Environment	Opportunity	Threat

ONE OF THE TOOLS YOU CAN USE TO ANALYZE YOUR CURRENT COMPANY SITUATION IS THE SWOT ANALYSIS.

TO DO THIS ANALYSIS, LET'S FIRST IDENTIFY YOUR SHOP'S STRENGTHS, WEAKNESSES, OPPORTUNITIES, AND THREATS.

■ SWOT

Strengths: Branding as an old, traditional shop, carefully chosen ingredients, made by a true craftsperson
Weaknesses: Small-scale business, limited production capacity
Opportunities: People concerned with food safety, preference for authenticity
Threats: Sudden price hike in ingredients, a decline in customers

I THINK THIS ABOUT DESCRIBES OUR CURRENT SITUATION.

LET'S FILL UP THE SWOT TABLE WITH THESE.

BY EXPLORING THESE, WE CAN SEE WHAT KIND OF STRATEGY TO TAKE.

LET'S TAKE A LOOK AT HOW PARTICULAR YOU ARE ABOUT YOUR INGREDIENTS, FOR EXAMPLE.

YOU USE CAREFULLY SELECTED HOKKAIDO INGREDIENTS AND YOUR MANJU IS MADE BY A SKILLED CRAFTSPERSON, SO IT'S GUARANTEED SAFE. UNLIKE YOUR RIVAL WHO ONLY GOT BIG MORE RECENTLY, YOUR SHOP HAS BEEN AROUND SINCE THE MEIJI ERA. IT'S AUTHENTIC FOR SURE.

THEN WHY DO YOU THINK CUSTOMERS DON'T STOP BY YOUR PLACE?

MAYBE BECAUSE THERE ARE MORE PEOPLE WHO DON'T KNOW THAT WE'RE AN OLD SHOP AND USE AUTHENTIC INGREDIENTS?

WHY THOUGH?

OH. I GUESS WE'RE PARTICULAR ABOUT HOW WE MAKE OUR MANJU ...

... BUT WE'VE NEVER REALLY BEEN PARTICULAR ABOUT HOW WE SELL IT.

EXACTLY! YOUR MARKETING IS WEAK!

NO, NOT EVEN! YOU HAVEN'T DONE ANY MARKETING AT ALL!

THAT MEANS THE FIRST STEP IS TO LEARN ABOUT MARKETING AND FORMULATE A STRATEGY!

I GOT THIS!

RIGHT AGAIN! THE CROSS-SWOT ANALYSIS EARLIER SHOULD TELL YOU WHAT STRATEGY YOU SHOULD TAKE NEXT!

ALL RIGHT! WHY DON'T WE GO AND PLAN OUR STRATEGY IN DETAIL?

YEAH!

KIZA BAKERY

EMO! GREAT JOB! SPLENDID!

THAT COPYCAT STRATEGY NAILED IT!

THINGS TURNED OUT AS I SAID, RIGHT? I WASN'T WRONG AFTER ALL!

HAHAHA! I LOOK FORWARD TO YOUR CONTINUED ASSISTANCE.

HEY! EMO!

SO CUTE! GIVE US A SMILE!

...

YES. NOW THAT I'M HERE, WE'LL CRUSH THAT PUNY LITTLE MANJU SHOP IN NO TIME.

HEY DAD, DON'T FORGET THAT ...

... I FOUND HIM!

HMM, I FEEL LIKE I GOT WHAT DIRECTION WE SHOULD BE TAKING FROM HERE.

...

BUT WE HAVE SO MANY OBSTACLES RIGHT NOW. CAN WE REALLY SAVE OUR SHOP?

1

Analyzing Your Customers, Your Competitors, and Your Company

As Logi explained to Marimo on page 105, you can analyze your business from three perspectives in marketing: customer analysis, competitor analysis, and company analysis. These three make up what is known as *3C analysis*. It is a widely used technique for breaking down company circumstances, formulating strategies, and reviewing plans.

Customer analysis: You look at statistics on your customers like their age, gender, profession, income, education, etc. You can also gather information about their lifestyle, purchase frequency, and their reasons for purchasing your product.

Competitor analysis: You analyze data you collect about your competitors. This also applies to other new companies that are planning to enter your market or companies that have a substitute product for one of yours.

Company analysis: You analyze your company's resources. It is important to know what resources you have and what position your company is occupying in the market. Company resources include human, financial, technical, and accumulated knowledge resources. For your company position, you will consider how well known you are to consumers, your brand strength, and your market share, among things.

3C Analysis

Analysis Target	Summary	Internal/ External
Customer	Here, you analyze your company's customers. You collect statistics like age, gender, occupation, income, education, and life stage. You also gather information on their lifestyle, personality, area of residence, buying frequency, reason for buying, etc. You then analyze these statistics and information.	External
Competitor	Here, you analyze businesses with competing brands and products. You should also analyze new companies entering the market or companies with products that could be a substitute for your own. Depending on the market, you may also have to consider other companies that appear to be from totally different fields. For example, a company that publishes weekly magazines will have to think of mobile phone and mobile gaming console companies as part of their competition.	External
Company	Here, you analyze the resources available to your company. You need to have an understanding of both your company resources and your company's position in the market. Company resources include human, financial, technical, and accumulated knowledge resources. For your position in the market, you analyze how well known your company is to consumers, your brand strength, and your market share, among things.	Internal

2

Identifying Your Company's Strengths, Weaknesses, External Opportunities, and Threats

SWOT (Strengths, Weaknesses, Opportunities, Threats) analysis is a very good tool if you want to focus on your company and analyze both your current internal conditions and any external threats. All companies have their strengths and weaknesses. Changes in the external surroundings of a company can then become opportunities for or threats to their business expansion.

In this analysis, you will first consider the internal strengths and weaknesses of your company. In the case of Tamaya, they can appeal to customers with their old traditional brand, their carefully chosen ingredients, and their professional craftsmanship. However, because of these same things, their production is limited and their cost rate is relatively high. As such, an external change that could become an opportunity for them would be increasing awareness of their products among people who prefer authentic products. On the other hand, the same authentic ingredients that inspire trust in their brand could become a threat if their prices suddenly rise. A decrease in their main customer base would also be a threat to their business.

Tamaya must also develop strategies to deal with their marketing weaknesses and the attacks from their big rival company.

Positive and Negative Factors from Internal and External Changes

	Positive Aspects	Negative Aspects
Originates from Internal Environment	Strength	Weakness
Originates from External Environment	Opportunity	Threat

SWOT Analysis for Tamaya

Strengths:
Branding as an old, traditional shop, carefully chosen ingredients, made by a true craftsperson

Weaknesses:
Small-scale business, limited production capacity

Opportunities:
People concerned with food safety, preference for authenticity

Threats:
Sudden price hike in ingredients, a decline in main customer base

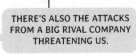

THEIR WEAK MARKETING ALSO GOES HERE.

THERE'S ALSO THE ATTACKS FROM A BIG RIVAL COMPANY THREATENING US.

Developing Strategies Based on Internal and External Factors

As it is, the SWOT analysis can only describe your company's current situation. To help in formulating plans and strategies, this analysis was improved into what is called Cross-SWOT analysis. In **Cross-SWOT analysis**, you organize the information on your opportunities, threats, strengths, and weaknesses into a matrix. By combining internal and external factors, this tool gives you a more strategic view that can help you plan your next steps.

For example, if you see a new opportunity where your strengths lie, you should develop a more aggressive and offensive plan. In addition, if you see changes in your external environment that could become a threat to your strengths, then you will want to take strategies to differentiate your product to avoid this risk. On the other side of all these, if you see a new opportunity that lies alongside your weaknesses, then you will want to find ways to conquer these weaknesses. If you see changes that can be a threat to your weaknesses, you will then want to think of strategies for retreating.

In Tamaya's case, they use carefully selected natural ingredients from Hokkaido and their manju is made by a skilled craftsperson. Because of this, they can appeal to customers with concerns about food safety. Compared to their rival, which is a much younger business, their shop has been around since the Meiji era. They should then be able to use their authenticity to appeal to consumers.

Cross-SWOT Analysis

Internal Environment		
	Strength	**Weakness**
Opportunity	**Aggressive Offensive Strategy** What kind of business opportunities can you use your strengths in?	**Step-by-Step Strategy** Are these opportunities that you could miss because of your weaknesses? What can you do to prevent this?
Threat	**Differentiation Strategy** Can you avoid these threats through your company's strengths? These may be threats to other companies, but can you instead use your company's strengths against these threats to differentiate yourself?	**Defensive Strategy** What effects could these threats to your company's weaknesses have? How do you defend against these effects?

Changes in External Environment

TRY THINKING ABOUT YOUR STRENGTHS, WEAKNESSES, OPPORTUNITIES, AND THREATS FROM AN OBSERVER'S POINT OF VIEW AND YOU MIGHT SEE MANY MORE OPTIONS TO PURSUE!

Building up on the Items Listed from Your SWOT Analysis

		Internal Environment	
		Company Strengths Branding as an old, traditional shop, carefully chosen ingredients, made by a true craftsperson	**Company Weaknesses** Small-scale business, limited production capacity, expensive, weak marketing
Changes in External Environment	**Opportunities** Demand for safe food, preference for authenticity	Fulfill existing demand for safe food and appeal as authentic	A marketing strategy to highlight that your production is limited because your product is authentic and uses only carefully selected ingredients
	Threats Price hike in ingredients, decline in customers, attack from rival company		

IT'S OF COURSE IMPORTANT TO IMPROVE AND CONQUER YOUR WEAKNESSES, BUT YOU CAN ALSO DEAL WITH THEM BY USING MORE POSITIVE WORDS TO DESCRIBE THEM OR BY CHANGING HOW YOU LOOK AT THEM!

Tamaya does have its strengths, and they should have had the chance to make use of these strengths. However, they weren't able to put their strengths together in a way to capitalize on available opportunities. Consequently, more and more people became unaware of their care for ingredients and their brand as an old, traditional shop. Tamaya is particular about how they make their manju, but they're not particular about how they sell them. That is, their marketing is weak and they lack business strategy. This is one conclusion you can draw from their situation.

Since they've arrived at this conclusion, they should be able to devise a more detailed business strategy that firmly makes use of their strengths and presents their weaknesses like their price and production limit in a positive light.

The SWOT analysis lets you understand your current circumstances, and, by doing a Cross-SWOT analysis, you can see what strategy you should be taking next for your particular situation.

The Five Force Model

The **Five Force Model** is a tool for understanding the forces in the industry that your company is a part of. The five competitive forces in an industry are (1) competitors in the industry, (2) new entrants to the industry, (3) the threat of substitute products, (4) the power of sellers as suppliers, and (5) the bargaining power of buyers. By looking at these five forces, you can determine how attractive an industry is for business.

For example, an industry might be growing, but this could mean that there are a lot of competitors and competition is fierce. This lowers the attractiveness of this industry. More new entrants to the industry would also mean that it would be harder to make a profit. On the other hand, an industry might be stagnant, but there could be less competition and fewer new companies coming into it. This could mean that it's easier to turn a profit in this industry with less effort.

By using the Five Force Model, you can identify which force is currently the most important for your company to tackle. You can then make use of the competition rules there to steer the industry in a direction that would be beneficial for your company.

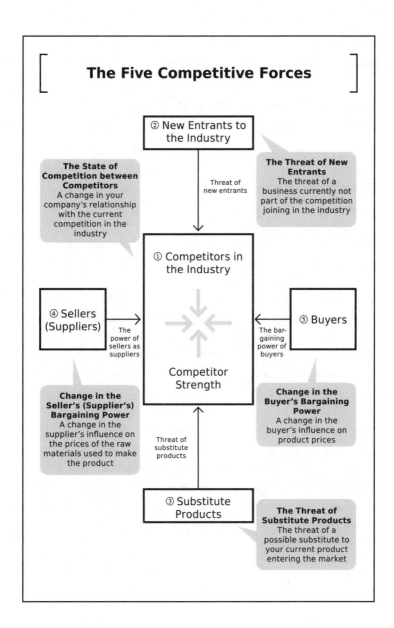

The Five Competitive Forces

② New Entrants to the Industry

The State of Competition between Competitors
A change in your company's relationship with the current competition in the industry

Threat of new entrants

The Threat of New Entrants
The threat of a business currently not part of the competition joining in the industry

① Competitors in the Industry

④ Sellers (Suppliers)

The power of sellers as suppliers

Competitor Strength

The bargaining power of buyers

⑤ Buyers

Change in the Seller's (Supplier's) Bargaining Power
A change in the supplier's influence on the prices of the raw materials used to make the product

Threat of substitute products

Change in the Buyer's Bargaining Power
A change in the buyer's influence on product prices

③ Substitute Products

The Threat of Substitute Products
The threat of a possible substitute to your current product entering the market

Deciding the Who, the What, and the How

Once you've identified what field your company focuses on through SWOT and other analyses, you can then decide on the domain your company should exist in. This is called your **strategic domain**.

You should ask yourself three questions in deciding your strategic domain. The first question is "Whom are you selling to?" This is the "who" question that identifies your target customers. The next question you should ask is "What are you selling?" This is the "what" question that identifies what your customer needs are. The last question is "How are you going to sell it?" This is the "how" question that aims to determine your company's distinctive competency.

This who, what, and how make up your strategic domain and are based on your internal strengths and weaknesses, external opportunities and threats. Once it becomes clear what your strategic domain is, it will become easier to formulate the more consistent, specific strategies and actual tactics you can use. Based on the strategic domain you've set, you can decide on your marketing policy. This covers what specific preparations you need to make and what resources, information, and funds you need to have on hand.

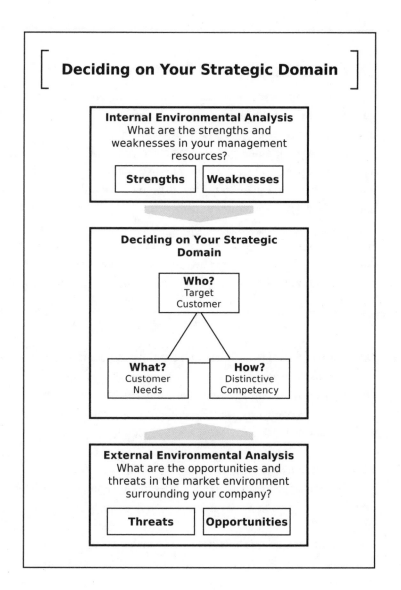

Deciding on Your Strategic Domain

Internal Environmental Analysis
What are the strengths and weaknesses in your management resources?

| Strengths | Weaknesses |

Deciding on Your Strategic Domain

Who?
Target Customer

What?
Customer Needs

How?
Distinctive Competency

External Environmental Analysis
What are the opportunities and threats in the market environment surrounding your company?

| Threats | Opportunities |

Different Marketing Strategies

Once you've decided what operations you'll be implementing for your company's growth and expansion, you will have to decide how you're going to compete with your competitors. Many different marketing strategies are available to you as you compete against other companies. Four representative ones are (1) imitation strategies, (2) market share strategies, (3) segmentation strategies, and (4) product differentiation strategies.

Imitation strategies are strategies in which you copy a leasing company's product in order to enter the market without having to take on the risks of new product development. In our story, the copycat strategy that Emo suggested to Kiza Bakery falls into this category.

Market share strategies are strategies focusing on your market share in a particular market. The most common example would be an expansion strategy where a company introduces a new product or increases its advertising budget in order to push for an increase in its market share.

In **segmentation strategies**, the market is divided into smaller segments and appropriate marketing activities are applied to each one.

Product differentiation strategies involve making your product distinctly superior to your competition and using this distinction to increase your market share. To avoid price competition, you will have to consider strategies other than your actual product strategies like your distribution and promotion strategies.

Four Types of Marketing Strategy

Strategy Type	Summary
Imitation Strategies	A strategy where you copy a leading company's product so you can enter the market without having to take on the risks of new product development. Representative examples are the three creative imitation strategies: the low-price strategy, the imitation innovation strategy, and the market power utilization strategy.
Market Share Strategies	Strategies that have to do with market share. A basic one is the share expansion strategy (increasing share) where a company introduces a new product or increases their advertising budget in order to increase their market share. There's also the market share preservation strategy (maintaining share) in which a company focuses on maintaining their current share. Along with the harvest strategy and strategic withdrawal, these make up the four market share strategies.
Segmentation Strategies	Strategies that first break your market into distinct components for analysis. In the market segmentation strategy, you divide the market into smaller segments based on some criteria and then find and implement the most effective marketing for each one. In the focus strategy, you pick a specific market segment and use the most optimal marketing for that. At present, most companies opt for the focus strategy because company resources are limited and may not be sufficient to work on multiple market segments at the same time.
Product Differentiation Strategies	Strategies that make your product distinctly superior to your competition. This distinction is used to increase your market share. In order to avoid price competition, you will have to consider strategies other than your actual product strategy, such as your distribution and promotion strategies.

Building a Competitive Edge

Based on the four types of marketing strategies, management guru Michael Porter proposed the **three generic strategies:** (1) the differentiation strategy, (2) the cost leadership strategy, and (3) the focus strategy. You can build your competitive edge using the most basic strategies: the **differentiation strategy** where you mainly use your product's uniqueness in order to differentiate yourself from other companies in the industry, and the **cost leadership strategy** where you concentrate on offering your product at a lower price than your competition by lowering the cost of production.

But there is a problem with using only these two strategies: Differentiating a product usually leads to higher development costs. In fact, differentiating your product will lead to a higher cost, but lowering the cost will make differentiation difficult.

Even so, this doesn't mean that only companies with the biggest market share can use these strategies. Even with a smaller share of the market, by narrowing down your target segment and using your limited resources wisely, you can build your competitive edge through a cost-focused or a differentiation-focused strategy.

In the story, Tamaya is trying to build their competitive edge against a big rival. You can probably say that going for a differentiation-focused strategy by differentiating their product for a small market segment is the natural course of action for their case.

Porter's Three Generic Strategies

Differentiation Strategy
A strategy that aims to build a competitive edge through product originality. Aside from technical quality, you can also differentiate a product by building a brand image or by offering quality service.

Cost Leadership Strategy
A strategy that aims to build a competitive edge by lowering manufacturing costs and offering products at lower prices than competitors. Suited for big companies that can more easily use scale to their advantage.

Bigger Segment

Differentiation Strategy	Cost Leadership Strategy
Focus Strategy	
Differentiation-Focused Strategy	Cost-Focused Strategy

Smaller Segment

Differentiation   Cost

Focus Strategy

Differentiation-Focused Strategy
A strategy that focuses on a specific target market to efficiently make use of limited resources. This applies the differentiation strategy to this specific target.

Cost-Focused Strategy
A strategy that focuses on a specific target market to efficiently make use of limited resources. This applies the cost leadership strategy to this specific target.

How You Fight the Battle Depends on Market Positioning

Philip Kotler's **competitive positioning strategy** looks at and organizes where companies are relative to each other in terms of competition. It's a tool for strategy formulation that's focused on management resources, which include human, physical, and information resources. Four strategies are plotted into a matrix, shown on the next page, based on the relative quality (high or low) and quantity (large or small) of your company's resources.

Leaders in the industry will focus on the expansion of the market as a whole and avoid competition with other companies. Challengers entering the market should aim to increase their share through differentiation and segmentation as they focus on a specific market. Market "nichers" focus on improving their techniques to produce a limited quantity of products that cater to a more limited market. Followers should try to imitate the success of market leaders and challengers by offering the same products at lower prices.

The strategy you should use will depend on the management resources that are available to your company.

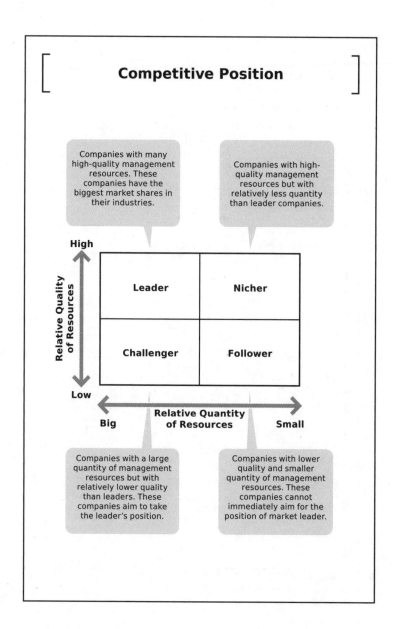

Competitive Position

Companies with many high-quality management resources. These companies have the biggest market shares in their industries.

Companies with high-quality management resources but with relatively less quantity than leader companies.

High

Relative Quality of Resources

| Leader | Nicher |
| Challenger | Follower |

Low

Big — **Relative Quantity of Resources** — Small

Companies with a large quantity of management resources but with relatively lower quality than leaders. These companies aim to take the leader's position.

Companies with lower quality and smaller quantity of management resources. These companies cannot immediately aim for the position of market leader.

Competitive Positioning Strategy

	Objective	State of the Company	Strategy
Leader	• Maintaining or increasing market share • Even greater profits • Wider recognition	• Has a large quantity of high-quality management resources • Has the biggest market share in the industry	Aims to expand the market as a whole and avoid competition with other companies in the industry
Challenger	• Increasing market share	• Has a large quantity of management resources but with relatively lower quality than leaders and aims to take the leader's position • Will usually aim for rank 2–4 in market share	• Has a large quantity of management resources but with relatively lower quality than leaders and aims to take the leader's position • Will usually aim for rank 2–4 in market share
Nicher	• Profit • Aims to be known in a specific market	• Has high-quality management resources but with relatively less quantity than leader companies	Unlike the leader, does not aim to produce a full line and a large quantity of products; instead, will target a specific market that's not in the leader's sights and use technical skills for that specific target
Follower	• Profit	• Has lower quality and smaller quantity of management resources	Imitates the success of market leaders and challengers by offering the same products that they offer but at lower prices

Part 5

Decide Who Your Customers Are

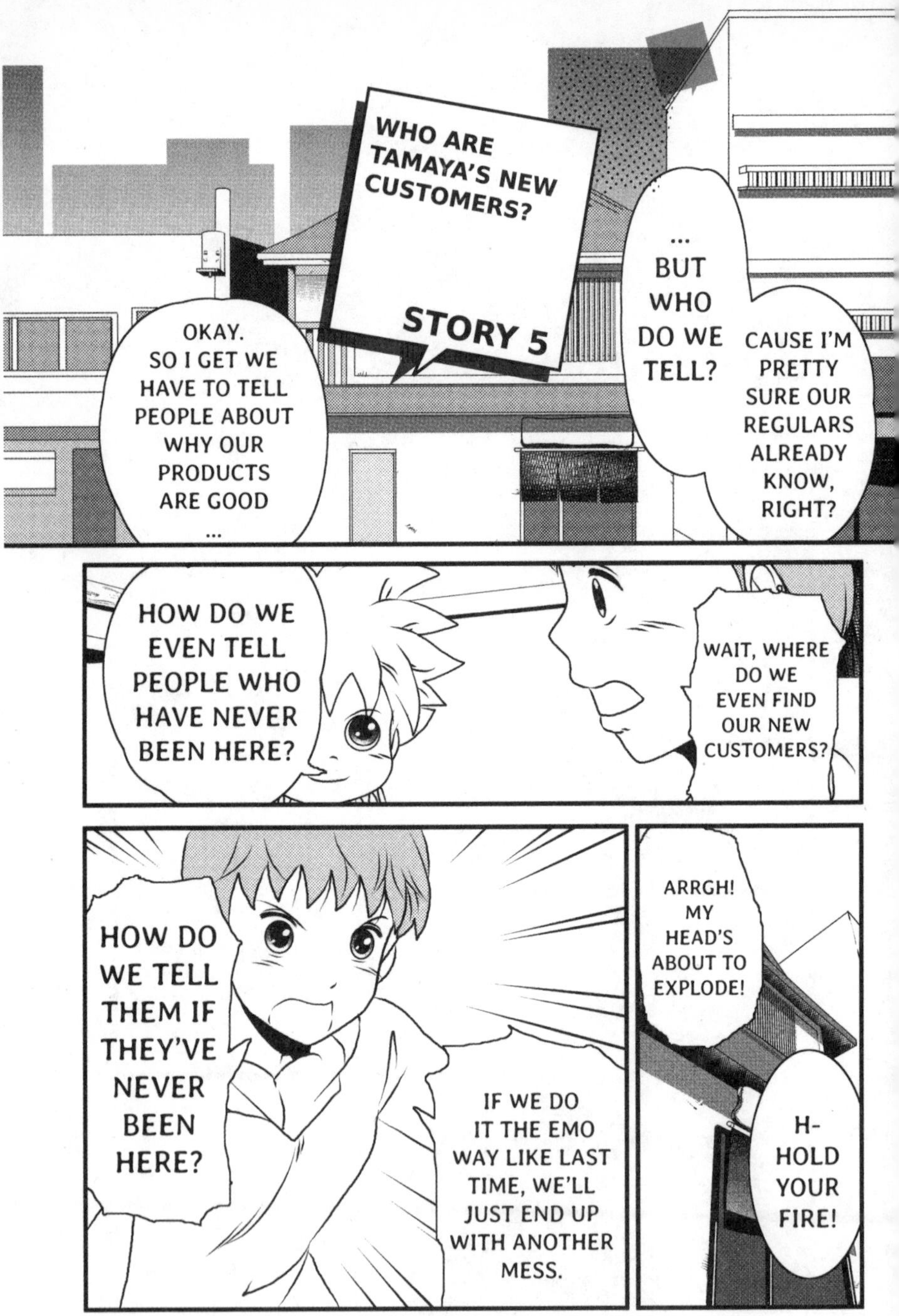
WHO ARE TAMAYA'S NEW CUSTOMERS?
STORY 5
OKAY. SO I GET WE HAVE TO TELL PEOPLE ABOUT WHY OUR PRODUCTS ARE GOOD ...
... BUT WHO DO WE TELL?
CAUSE I'M PRETTY SURE OUR REGULARS ALREADY KNOW, RIGHT?
HOW DO WE EVEN TELL PEOPLE WHO HAVE NEVER BEEN HERE?
WAIT, WHERE DO WE EVEN FIND OUR NEW CUSTOMERS?
HOW DO WE TELL THEM IF THEY'VE NEVER BEEN HERE?
IF WE DO IT THE EMO WAY LIKE LAST TIME, WE'LL JUST END UP WITH ANOTHER MESS.
ARRGH! MY HEAD'S ABOUT TO EXPLODE!
H- HOLD YOUR FIRE!

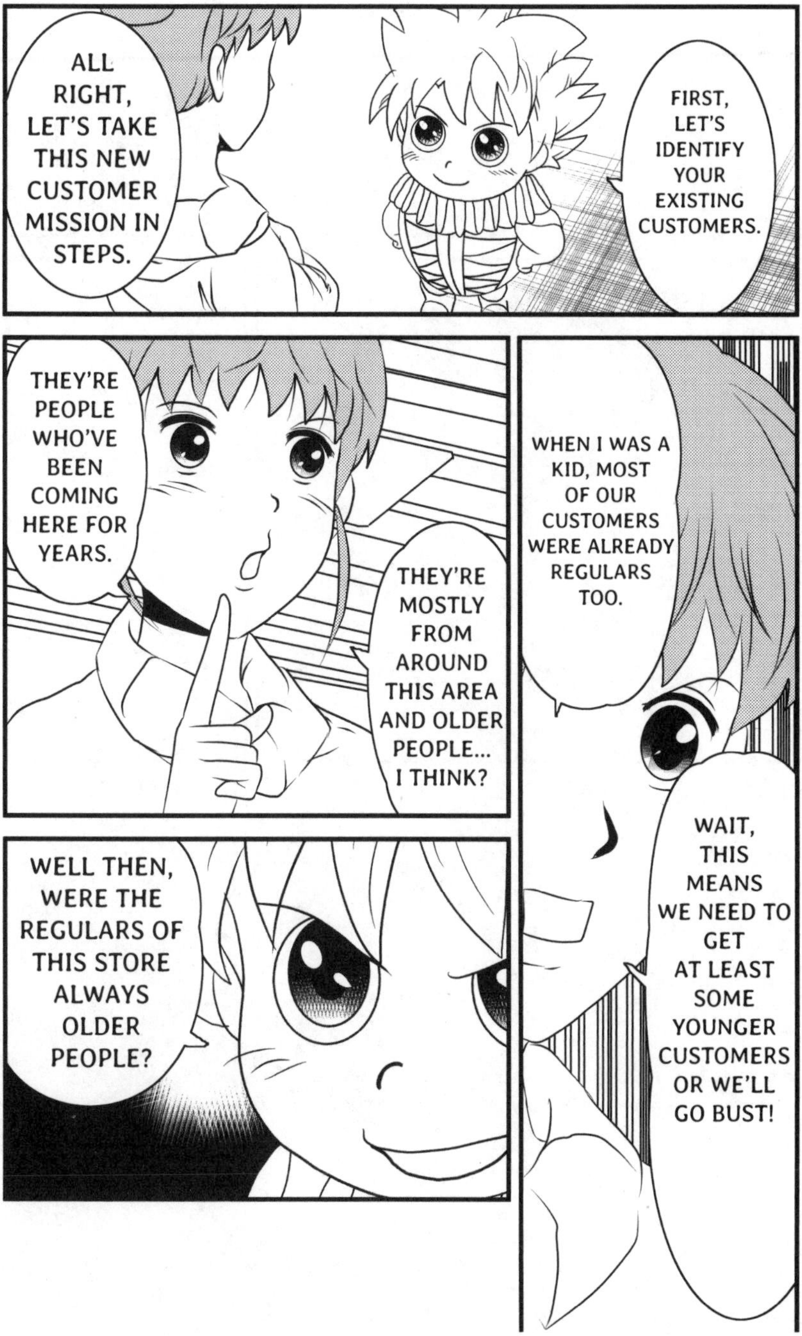
ALL RIGHT, LET'S TAKE THIS NEW CUSTOMER MISSION IN STEPS.
FIRST, LET'S IDENTIFY YOUR EXISTING CUSTOMERS.
THEY'RE PEOPLE WHO'VE BEEN COMING HERE FOR YEARS.
THEY'RE MOSTLY FROM AROUND THIS AREA AND OLDER PEOPLE... I THINK?
WHEN I WAS A KID, MOST OF OUR CUSTOMERS WERE ALREADY REGULARS TOO.
WELL THEN, WERE THE REGULARS OF THIS STORE ALWAYS OLDER PEOPLE?
WAIT, THIS MEANS WE NEED TO GET AT LEAST SOME YOUNGER CUSTOMERS OR WE'LL GO BUST!

JUST "YOUNGER PEOPLE" STILL COVERS TOO WIDE A SCOPE. WE NEED TO NARROW IT DOWN.

IF TOO MANY DIFFERENT KINDS OF YOUNGER PEOPLE COME HERE, THE ATMOSPHERE OF YOUR STORE WILL BE ALL OVER THE PLACE AND YOUR BOOM WILL END UP SHORT-LIVED LIKE THE LAST TIME.

OH, WE HAD THOSE SIBLINGS LAST TIME, DIDN'T WE? THE ONES WHO GOT MANJU FOR THEIR GRANDMA.

I THINK IT'D BE NICE TO HAVE THAT KIND OF FAMILY THEME. LIKE SOMETHING THAT CAN BE WITH OUR CUSTOMERS WHILE THEY SPEND QUALITY TIME WITH FAMILY.

THEN I'LL TEACH YOU HOW TO IDENTIFY WHAT GROUP YOU SHOULD AIM FOR THROUGH STP MARKETING.

STP MARKETING?

STP STANDS FOR SEGMENTATION, TARGETING, AND POSITIONING.

Group your market according to customer needs.

S
SEGMENTATION

Decide on your product's position.

Narrow down the market you're going for.

T
TARGETING

P
POSITIONING

FIRST, LET'S THINK ABOUT YOUR SPECIALTY, THE MARIMO MANJU.

YOU ALREADY HAVE A PRODUCT YOU'RE TRYING TO SELL, SO LET'S DO PROUCT-BASED SEGMENTATION AND TARGETING.

WHAT'S SPECIAL ABOUT YOUR PRODUCT?

IT'S AUTHENTIC AND ALL THE INGREDIENTS ARE SAFE.

PLUS, IT'S A TRADITIONAL JAPANESE SWEET, SO IT GOES WELL WITH TEA.

NEXT, WHAT KIND OF CUSTOMERS DO YOU WANT TO HAVE?

WHO WOULD YOU LIKE TO SELL YOUR MARIMO MANJU TO?

HMM.

WHEN WE FOLLOWED EMO'S PLAN, WE GOT A LOT OF DIFFERENT CUSTOMERS.

TRY TO REMEMBER WHAT KIND OF PEOPLE THEY WERE.

ON WEEKDAYS, WE GOT COUPLES AND YOUNGER NON-WORKING GROUPS.

WE ALSO GOT HOMEMAKERS AND SOME OFFICE WORKERS WHO SEEM TO BE BUYING TO EAT IT AT THEIR WORKPLACE.

IN THE EVENING, WE HAD PEOPLE ON THEIR WAY HOME FROM WORK.

THERE WERE ALSO PEOPLE OUT ON A DRIVE WITH THEIR FAMILIES.

135

RIGHT. YOU HAD MANY DIFFERENT CUSTOMERS.

YOUNG AND SINGLE GROUP

FAMILY GROUP

SENIOR CITIZEN GROUP

TEENAGER GROUP

FOR EXAMPLE, THERE WERE YOUNG SINGLES, FAMILIES, SENIORS, AND TEENAGERS. GROUPING THEM LIKE THIS IS WHAT YOU CALL SEGMENTATION.

WHO DO YOU THINK AMONG THESE PEOPLE WOULD MORE LIKELY REGULARLY COME TO BUY YOUR MARIMO MANJU?

THE TEEN-AGERS TENDED TO COME HERE ONLY ONCE.

COMPARED TO CHOCOLATES AND OTHER SNACKS, OUR MANJU HAS A SHORTER SHELF LIFE, SO YOUNG SINGLES WHO LIVE ALONE CAN'T EASILY STOCK AND EAT IT.

IN THAT CASE, SINCE THEY NORMALLY HAVE TEA EVERY DAY ...

SENIOR CITIZEN GROUP

... IT SEEMS OUR MAIN TARGET IS THE SENIORS.

DOES THIS MEAN WE CAN'T TARGET THE FAMILY GROUP LIKE THOSE KIDS BEFORE?

I GUESS IT MIGHT BE DIFFICULT IF WE DO THE PRODUCT-BASED APPROACH.

OH, BUT THEY'VE BEEN DEVELOPING RESIDENTIAL AREAS ALL AROUND HERE, SO I THINK THERE ARE MORE FAMILIES NOW.

I WANT TO TARGET THIS GROUP. FOOD SAFETY AND SECURITY ARE PROBABLY VALUABLE TO PARENTS TOO.

AND JUST LIKE FOR THOSE KIDS, THERE'S A CHANCE OF CONNECTING TO THEIR GRAND-PARENTS TOO.

IN THAT CASE, LET'S GO WITH A MARKET-BASED APPROACH WHERE YOU HAVE A TARGET AND WANT TO DEVELOP A PRODUCT FOR IT.

YOUR TARGET IS THE FAMILY SEGMENT!

THAT MEANS YOU HAVE TO DEVELOP A PRODUCT THAT THE FAMILY SEGMENT WILL WANT!

THAT MEANS TAMAYA'S CURRENT SPECIALTY IS TOO WEAK TO APPEAL TO THE FAMILY GROUP.

WE'RE UNEARTHING ONE WEAKNESS OF THIS SHOP AFTER ANOTHER.

IN SHORT!

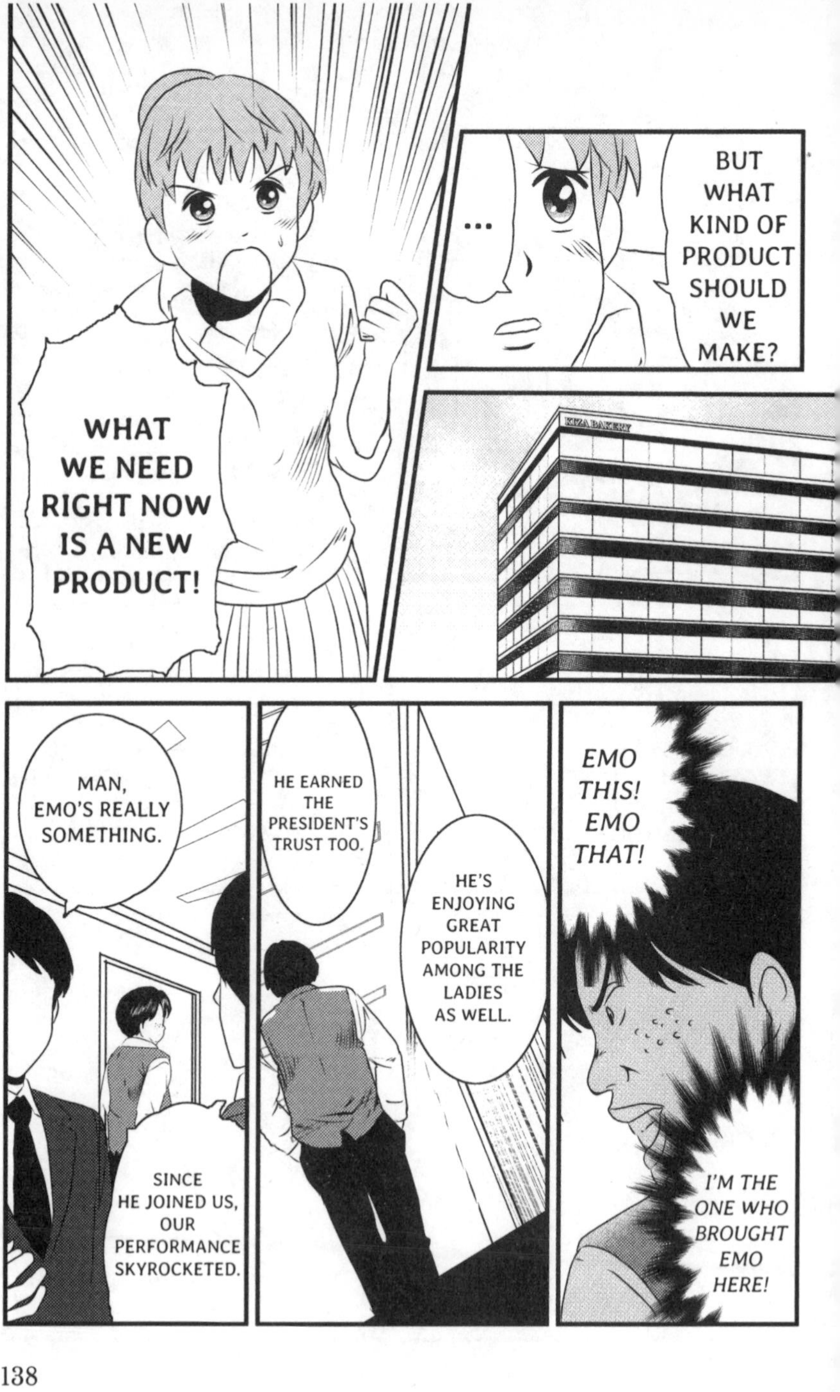
WHAT WE NEED RIGHT NOW IS A NEW PRODUCT!
...
BUT WHAT KIND OF PRODUCT SHOULD WE MAKE?
KIZA BAKERY
MAN, EMO'S REALLY SOMETHING.
SINCE HE JOINED US, OUR PERFORMANCE SKYROCKETED.
HE EARNED THE PRESIDENT'S TRUST TOO.
HE'S ENJOYING GREAT POPULARITY AMONG THE LADIES AS WELL.
EMO THIS! EMO THAT!
I'M THE ONE WHO BROUGHT EMO HERE!

OW!

BAM

WHAT WAS THAT FOR?!

YOUR JOB HERE'S DONE, PUNK. I JUST WANTED TO CORNER MARIMO'S SHOP.

HA HA HA !

I'LL TAKE OVER FROM HERE. I DON'T NEED YOU ANY-MORE!

OH YEAH, WHERE'S EMO?

I KNOW! WE'RE ABOUT TO GET BUSY HERE! WHERE'D HE WANDER OFF TO?!

139

Connecting Product and Customer: The STP Marketing Model

In order to sell your product, you will need to decide what kind of product you want to sell to which consumers and in which market. You will also need to select the image you want to attach to the product. This section will be about the **STP (Segmentation, Targeting, and Positioning) Marketing Model,** which is a tool that you can use to connect your product with your customers.

In solidifying your STP, you need to be aware of both the product-based and the market-based approaches that Logi talked about in the manga. Different companies will have to work with different circumstances in selling their products. If your company has to sell an existing or previously developed product no matter what, then you should take a product-based approach in thinking about your STP.

On the other hand, if you don't have a particular product to sell or if your company is going to start from product development, then taking the market-based approach is more appropriate. In this approach, you'll look for and choose a promising market first; then you'll choose or develop a product that would sell in that market. **It's very important to be able to tell when to use the product-based approach, where you decide on a market for an already existing product, or the market-based approach, in which you decide on a product for a promising market.**

The Segmentation Process and the Two Approaches to STP

Step	Process	Summary
STEP 1	Deciding on a target market	Based on the pros, decide on your approach and marketing mix.
STEP 2	Deciding on a variable for segmentation	Decide on how to slice out your target market with its particular needs.
STEP 3	Outlining the segments	Outline the segments based on demographics, geographic variables, and the buyer's actions and reactions.
STEP 4	Deciding which segment to aim for	Based on your company resources and competition situation, narrow down the segment into one with the best size and best chances.
STEP 5	Making a marketing plan	Based on your plan thus far, refine your implementation plan.

Approach	Situation	Next Steps
Product-based	You have an existing product that you want to expand to another market.	First, decide on a target through segmentation and adjust the concept of your product to fit with your target. Look at your available products and think of and build a product concept that your chosen target will probably like. Then you'll change the positioning of your product to match this.
Market-based	You have to first confirm the existence of a market before developing your product.	In developing a new product, first, you have to think about what kind of customer buys a product and why. A useful tool here is the positioning map. By mapping out the different standards that consumers use in their heads, you can find the market with unfulfilled needs.

Finding Common Factors among Similar Consumers

Segmentation is of course important when you're developing a new product, but it becomes even more important when you already have a developed product and you're going to use the product-based approach to marketing.

With many fields already crowded with companies and with the diversification in consumer lifestyles, the needs and wants of customers cannot be satisfied with just one product. Consequently, most companies narrow their target and develop their business based on that. To differentiate their products from the competition, companies divide consumers into groups and target only one group to expand their business.

This process of dividing the market into groups is called **segmentation**, and each group is called a **segment**. This is a very important factor in connecting your customers with your product and company. Even if you have a good product or service, if you pick the wrong segment to sell to, you won't be able to make them happily buy your product.

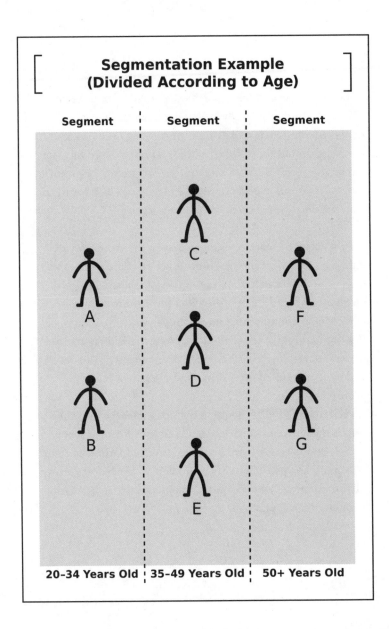

Segmentation Example
(Divided According to Age)

Segment	Segment	Segment

20-34 Years Old | 35-49 Years Old | 50+ Years Old

In the story, Logi divided Tamaya's customers into the young and single group, the family group, the senior citizen group, and the teenager group. Just like this, by imagining, studying, and observing the customers who use your company's product, you will also be able to divide them into groups. By picking the group you want to offer your product or service to, you can then formulate strategies and tactics that fit with that group.

Using your segmentation results to narrow the group you are selling to is called **targeting**. Three targeting approaches can be used: (1) **undifferentiated marketing**, in which you disregard the segments and develop the market the same way for all segments; (2) **differentiated marketing**, in which you approach each segment with a segment-appropriate marketing mix; and (3) **focused marketing**, in which you pick one segment and develop a marketing mix suited for that particular segment only.

Most companies today choose to do focused marketing. They concentrate on a market that matches their company's scope and do their best to raise their sales there. Just like Marimo and Emo, you should first pick a type of customer who seems like they will respond well to your approach and develop strategies and promotions appropriate for that group.

Three Types of Targeting

- **Undifferentiated Marketing**

Market (All Males)	←	Marketing Mix

- **Differentiated Marketing**

Segment (Males aged 20-34)	←	Marketing Mix
Segment (Males aged 35-49)	←	Marketing Mix
Segment (Males aged 50 and above)	←	Marketing Mix

- **Focused Marketing**

Segment (Males aged 20-34)	←	Marketing Mix
Segment (Males aged 35-49)		
Segment (Males aged 50 and above)		

Segmentation can be based on different variables like **geographic variables**, which are based on where people live; **demographic variables** like age and gender; **social and psychological variables**, which include lifestyle and values; and **behavioral variables** like purchase frequency. You can pick the classification variable most suited to your particular case to divide your market.

Furthermore, dividing the market according to what customers buy is called *market segmentation*, while dividing up your customers according to what they're like is called *customer segmentation*.

Appropriately segmenting your market, developing products to fulfill your market's needs, and building suitable marketing strategies are likely to lead to the success of your product.

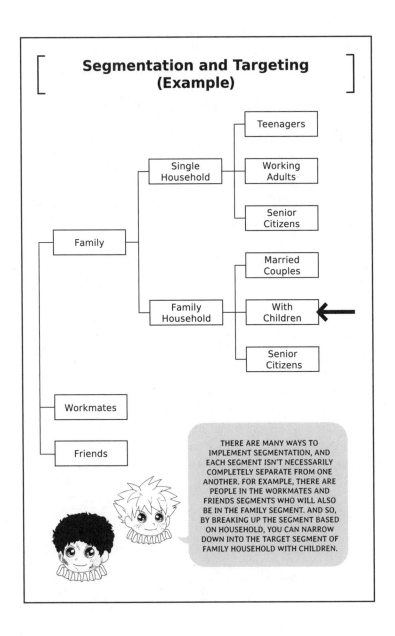

Segmentation and Targeting (Example)

THERE ARE MANY WAYS TO IMPLEMENT SEGMENTATION, AND EACH SEGMENT ISN'T NECESSARILY COMPLETELY SEPARATE FROM ONE ANOTHER. FOR EXAMPLE, THERE ARE PEOPLE IN THE WORKMATES AND FRIENDS SEGMENTS WHO WILL ALSO BE IN THE FAMILY SEGMENT. AND SO, BY BREAKING UP THE SEGMENT BASED ON HOUSEHOLD, YOU CAN NARROW DOWN INTO THE TARGET SEGMENT OF FAMILY HOUSEHOLD WITH CHILDREN.

Mapping Consumer Perception

Positioning deals with where your product would stand if a customer decides to compare it with other competitors' products. Positioning is important when you already have a product you want to sell, but it becomes especially important when you use the market-based approach where you first look for a market and then develop a product targeted at that market.

In developing a new product, you first have to ask what kind of customers buy a product and for what purpose. An especially useful tool for this is the **positioning map**. By actually mapping out the comparison standards in a customer's mind, you can find which market has unfulfilled needs.

As an example, I made a positioning map for the car market. This map is based on car size, which relates to the environment, easy city driving, and spaciousness on the inside, which relates to comfort and coziness. In the older positioning map, you will notice that the lower right space was vacant. The product that was developed to target this space is the now popular compact car.

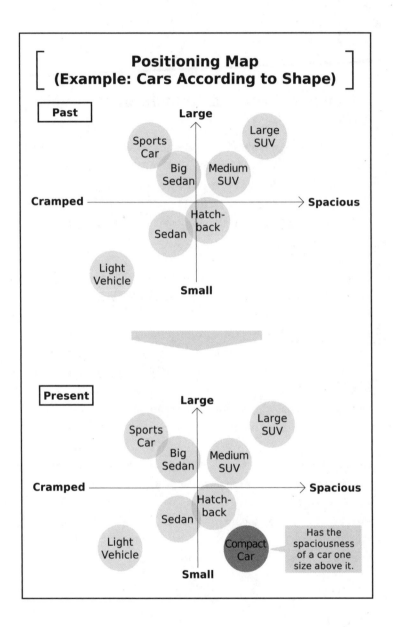

Positioning Map
(Example: Cars According to Shape)

Past

Large

Sports Car

Big Sedan

Medium SUV

Large SUV

Cramped ————————————→ Spacious

Hatch-back

Sedan

Light Vehicle

Small

Present

Large

Sports Car

Big Sedan

Medium SUV

Large SUV

Cramped ————————————→ Spacious

Hatch-back

Sedan

Light Vehicle

Compact Car

Has the spaciousness of a car one size above it.

Small

Decide Who Your Customers Are   Part 5   149

Changing Your Target Changes Your Concept

A **product concept** is a backbone idea that's used to maintain consistency for a product from manufacturing to sale. When developing a new product in the market-based approach, a target and position are decided using the position map among other tools, and along with these, the product concept is taken into the development process.

However, in the product-based approach where you're introducing an existing product into a different market, you first set a target through segmentation, then adjust the product concept to match that new target. You view the existing product and come up with a concept for it according to your new target market's preferences. This process also changes the position of your product. **You need to keep your target, position, and product concept all closely related and make adjustments while maintaining consistency between the three of them.**

In the coffee beverage example on page 153, you will find different concept examples that were made to match the different target markets. Once you find the concept that matches each target, you'll then have to work on the new product name, packaging and size, sales route, and price. You may also have to add some ingredients to change its taste to match the concept.

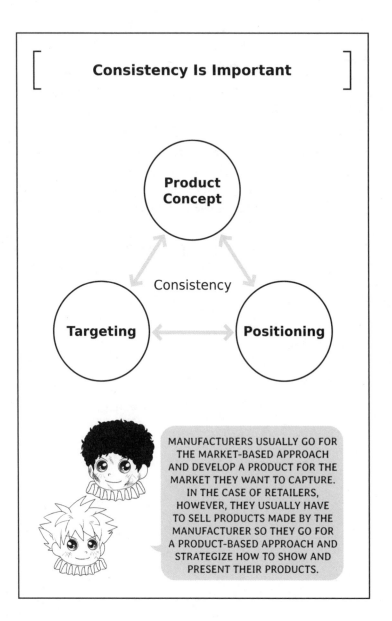

Consistency Is Important

Product Concept

Consistency

Targeting

Positioning

MANUFACTURERS USUALLY GO FOR THE MARKET-BASED APPROACH AND DEVELOP A PRODUCT FOR THE MARKET THEY WANT TO CAPTURE. IN THE CASE OF RETAILERS, HOWEVER, THEY USUALLY HAVE TO SELL PRODUCTS MADE BY THE MANUFACTURER SO THEY GO FOR A PRODUCT-BASED APPROACH AND STRATEGIZE HOW TO SHOW AND PRESENT THEIR PRODUCTS.

There are cases of product-based development where the product you're selling and the ingredients you can use are already set. There are also cases where you'll do a market-based approach where your target is already decided or has to be decided based on your standpoint, market scope, and sales route. Many different situations surround business and commerce and will dictate how your product concept, target, and position may change over time.

Once you've confirmed the consistency of your product's concept, target, and position, you will then decide on the more detailed elements of your product. We will learn about the marketing mix in the next part, which combines all the elements needed to be decided for your product.

Changing Your Target Changes Your Concept

Target	Concept (Example: Coffee Beverage)
Company Workers (Morning)	For mornings; wakes you up
Seniors	A coffee that goes well with Japanese food and sweets
Heavy Coffee Drinkers	Less caffeine
Office Workers	A beverage to help you relax before a big presentation
Manual Laborers	Gives you that afternoon energy for work
Young Women	A diet support drink that increases your metabolism and helps burn fat
Athletes	Helps you concentrate and prevents muscle pain
Drivers	A cup to help you wake up
Stressed People	Helps fight depression and spikes motivation
Middle-aged Men	Effective against hangover headaches
Middle-aged Women	Fights free radicals that accelerate aging

A General Rule for Narrowing Down Your Target Consumers

There is a segmentation rule that you should follow when choosing your market. When these four conditions are not met, you will have segmented for nothing as you can't use your segments for your actual marketing strategy. You will get stuck in market research and will end up wasting both time and money.

Make sure to check these four conditions not only during segmentation but during the market research step that comes before it.

- **Market Segmentation Rule**

Rule	Question	Bad Example
Measurability	Can it be measured?	For example, if you make a segment for people who are "Big Fans of Cars," people have different ways of valuing cars. Because of this, you will get wildly different answers for what type of car they like or what they're looking for in a car and the measurement of the market itself becomes difficult.
Reachability	Can you really approach your chosen segments?	Even if you consider the country's statistical definition of the rich, if you don't know where people who fit this definition are, you can't approach them. If you can't contact them in any way, then you can't do business with them.
Maintainability	Is there a big enough market? (Profit, response, long-term stability)	If you choose a niche market that doesn't fall under repeat sales and your target market is too small, you cannot make enough sales and profit to guarantee the continued existence of your company.
Implementability	Can this be implemented?	Even if you want to target people all over the world who are fans of Japan's healthy food and try to sell them natural Japanese ingredients, you'll find that the cost and logistics for shipping these goods will make it practically unfeasible to implement.

Part 6

Deciding Your 4 Ps

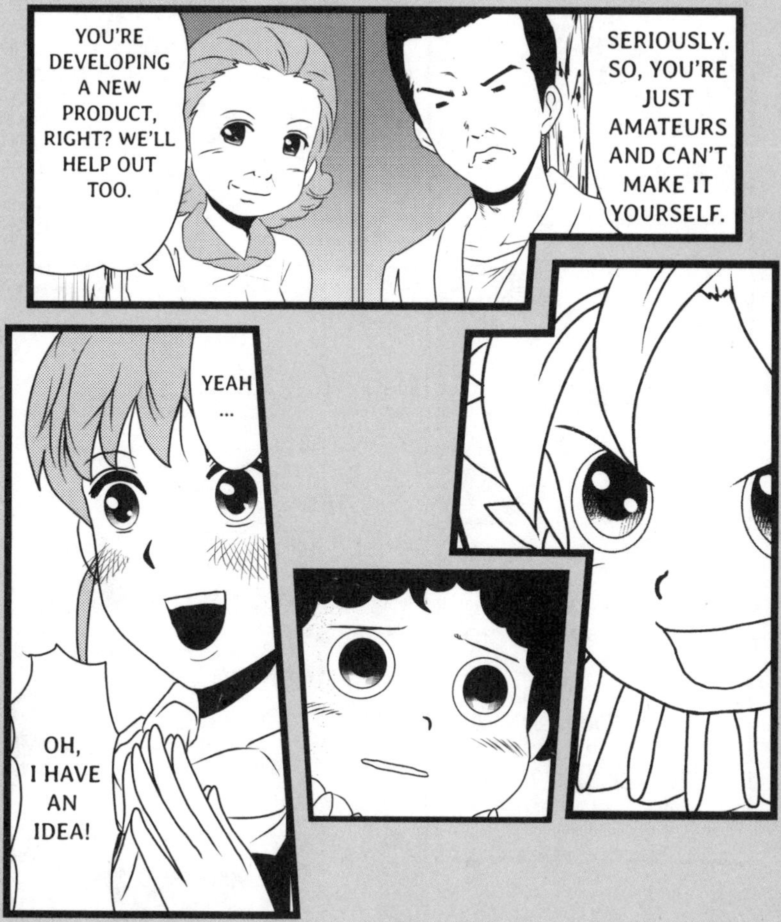

YOU'RE DEVELOPING A NEW PRODUCT, RIGHT? WE'LL HELP OUT TOO.
SERIOUSLY. SO, YOU'RE JUST AMATEURS AND CAN'T MAKE IT YOURSELF.
YEAH ...
OH, I HAVE AN IDEA!

THE SHORT BOOM IN OUR SALES HAS NOW PASSED ...

LET'S MAKE MINI MARIMO MANJU!

STORY 6

... AND WITH OUR REGULARS COMING BACK, OUR STORE IS BACK TO ITS PREVIOUS QUIET AND EMPTY STATE.

IF THERE IS A RAY OF HOPE TO BE SEEN HERE...

I THINK I'M BEGINNING TO UNDERSTAND MARKETING MORE AND MORE.

IT'S LIKE THE SEPARATE IDEAS I LEARNED BEFORE ARE NOW STARTING TO CONNECT.

ALL THAT'S LEFT NOW IS TO DEVELOP A NEW PRODUCT...!

...IT'S THAT SOME OF THE YOUNG FAMILIES WHO FOUND OUT ABOUT TAMAYA THROUGH THAT BOOM HAVE NOW BECOME REPEAT CUSTOMERS.

...THAT WILL HELP US SECURE THESE NEW CUSTOMERS!

MARI-MO! YOU HAVE A CALL.

IT'S FROM YAMAZAKI IN TOKYO!

?

OKAJIMA TOLD ME TO CALL YOU HERE. I'M SURPRISED THAT YOU'RE TAKING SUCH A LONG LEAVE! I'M SORRY, THERE'S BEEN A MISUNDERSTANDING. I DIDN'T REALLY MEAN THAT YOU'RE FIRED.

CHIEF!

WHY DON'T YOU COME BACK TO WORK?

ABOUT YOUR PROJECT... IT'S TRUE THAT THERE ARE STILL THINGS THAT NEED TO BE FIXED, BUT WE CAN STILL TAKE A LOOK AT IT TOGETHER.

CHIEF...

THANK GOODNESS... I GUESS I WASN'T ABANDONED YET...

BUT...

CHIEF, I'M SORRY. PLEASE JUST GIVE ME A BIT MORE TIME.

I FEEL LIKE I'M CLOSE TO LEARNING SOMETHING IMPORTANT HERE!

UP UNTIL NOW, I'VE ONLY EVER WORKED WITH A SELF-CENTERED MINDSET.

EVEN IF I GO BACK TO WORK NOW, I'LL JUST REPEAT MY MISTAKES.

I LEARNED THAT YOU NEED TO USE VARIOUS METHODS AND IDEAS TO MAKE THE PARTY YOU'RE DEALING WITH HAPPY.

CLICK

I WANT TO FIND AN ANSWER MYSELF BEFORE I GO BACK TO WORK.

I WANT TO THINK OF A PRODUCT—OF AN ANSWER—AND DERIVE THE SOLUTION FROM THERE!

MARIMO.

158

SERIOUSLY. SO, YOU'RE JUST AMATEURS AND CAN'T MAKE IT YOURSELF.

YOU'RE DEVELOPING A NEW PRODUCT, RIGHT? WE'LL HELP OUT TOO.

I DON'T GET ALL THE DIFFICULT WORDS, BUT I GET THAT YOU'RE SINCERELY THINKING OF OUR STORE.

IF THAT'S THE CASE, THEN LET ME HELP OUT.

YOUR DAD'S FINALLY REALIZED YOUR HARD WORK! LET'S THINK ABOUT THIS TOGETHER.

MOM. DAD.

LET'S DO IT!

THAT'S RIGHT. WE'LL ALL WORK TOGETHER TO CREATE A NEW PRODUCT!

Tamaya

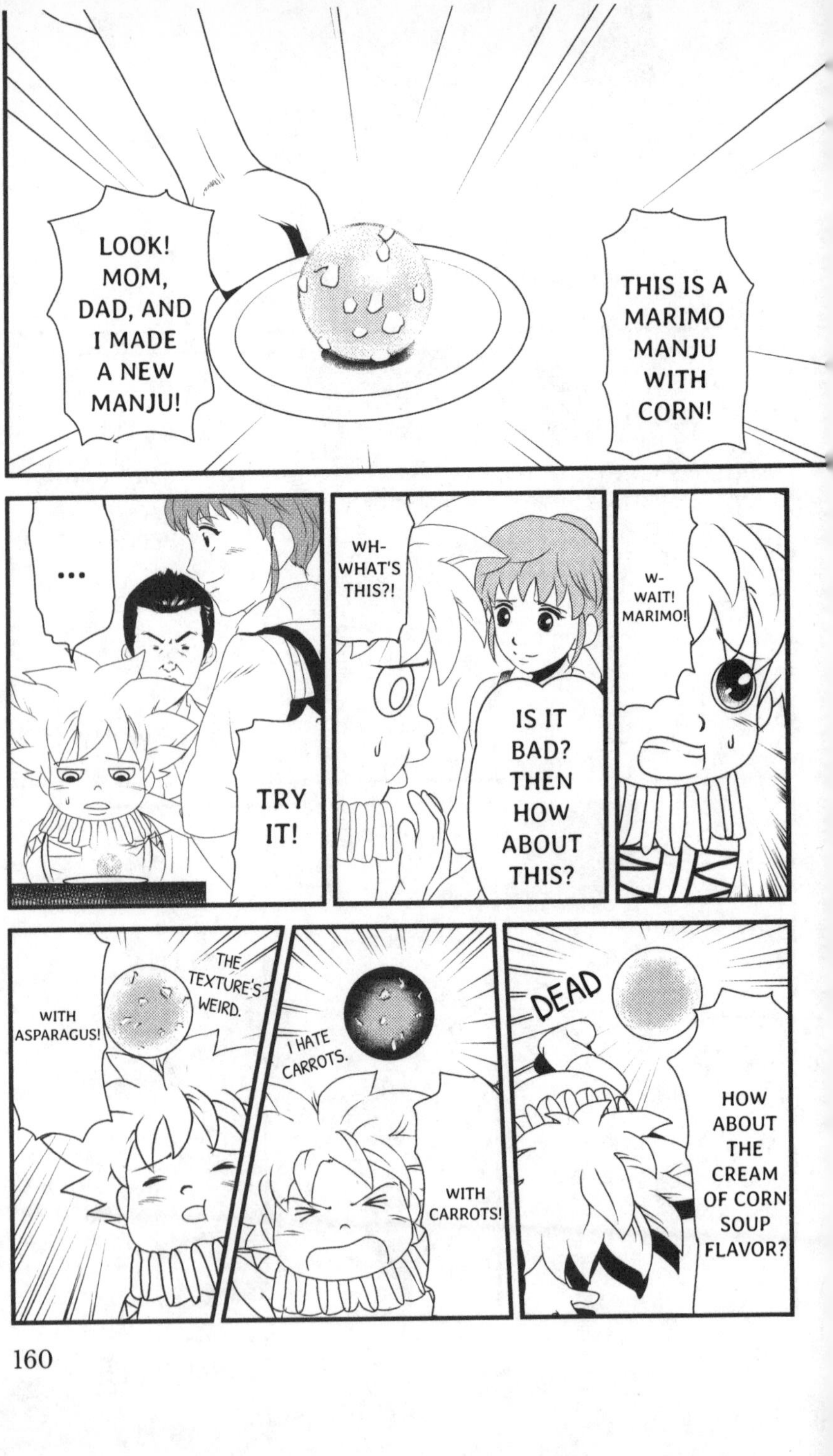
LOOK! MOM, DAD, AND I MADE A NEW MANJU!
THIS IS A MARIMO MANJU WITH CORN!
...
TRY IT!
WH- WHAT'S THIS?!
IS IT BAD? THEN HOW ABOUT THIS?
W- WAIT! MARIMO!
WITH ASPARAGUS!
THE TEXTURE'S WEIRD.
WITH CARROTS!
I HATE CARROTS.
HOW ABOUT THE CREAM OF CORN SOUP FLAVOR?
DEAD

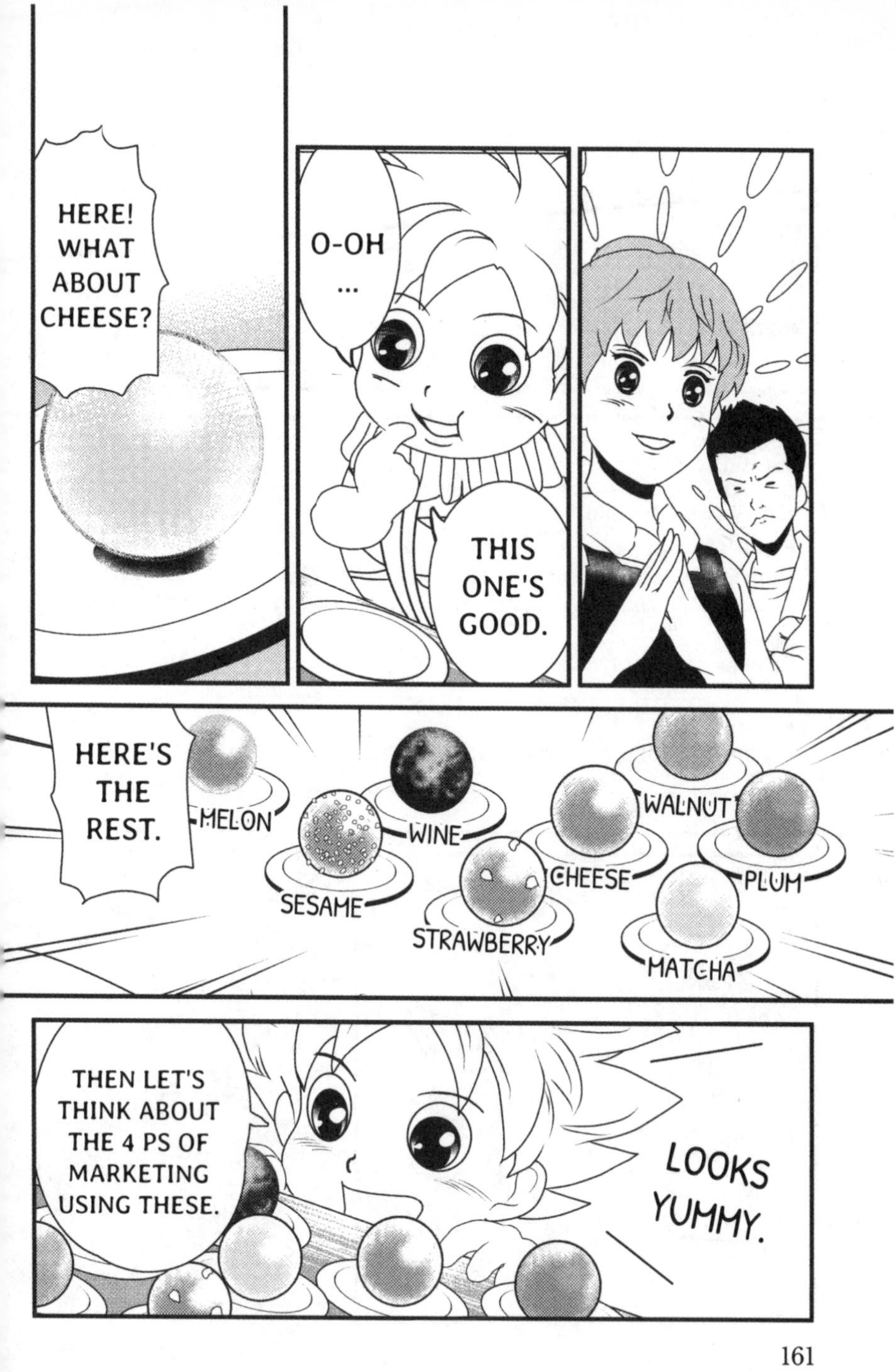
HERE! WHAT ABOUT CHEESE?
O-OH ...
THIS ONE'S GOOD.
HERE'S THE REST.
MELON
SESAME
WINE
STRAWBERRY
CHEESE
WALNUT
PLUM
MATCHA
THEN LET'S THINK ABOUT THE 4 PS OF MARKETING USING THESE.
LOOKS YUMMY.

Product
Quality, type of product, design, unique features, brand name, packaging, size, service, warranty, product returns

Price
Target price, discount, golden handcuffs, payment period, credit terms

Place
Channel, transport, inventory, scope of circulation, location, lineup

Promotion
Communication mix (sales, advertising, and promotion), sales staff, direct marketing, online marketing

PRODUCT

HMM. HOW DO WE USE THESE NEW MANJU TO CAPTURE THE NEW CUSTOMERS WHO WERE DIFFICULT TO CAPTURE WITH JUST YOUR CURRENT SPECIALTY? I THINK EACH IS PRETTY WEAK ON ITS OWN, SO...

...HOW ABOUT WE OFFER ALL THESE ASSORTED FLAVORS AS A SET?

BUT WITH THIS SIZE, EATING JUST ONE IS ALREADY PRETTY FILLING.

THEN WE CAN MAKE IT SMALLER.

HOW ABOUT WE MAKE THEM BITE-SIZED SO YOU CAN EAT ALL THE DIFFERENT FLAVORS?

WE CAN ALSO MAKE OUR SPECIAL MARIMO MANJU SMALLER AND ADD IT TO THE MIX. THAT WAY, EVERYONE FROM THE GRANDPARENTS TO THE PARENTS TO THE GRANDKIDS CAN ALL ENJOY THEM TOGETHER.

THEY CAN EVEN PLAY GAMES TO DECIDE WHO GETS WHICH FLAVOR. IT CAN EVEN HELP START CONVERSATIONS!

YEAH...

OH, I HAVE AN IDEA!

163

HOW ABOUT A BIRTHDAY PACKAGE? WE'LL WRAP THEM UP IN A ROUND BOX LIKE A CAKE!

!

THEN EVERYONE CAN PICK WHATEVER THEY LIKE WHILE HAVING FUN!

MAYBE THEY CAN ALSO BE A SUBSTITUTE FOR PARTY FAVORS AT WEDDINGS.

RIGHT. THERE'S SOMETHING VERY IMPORTANT YOU NEED TO KNOW.

THERE ARE THREE POINTS YOU NEED TO KEEP IN MIND TO DIFFERENTIATE WHEN YOU THINK ABOUT A NEW PRODUCT.

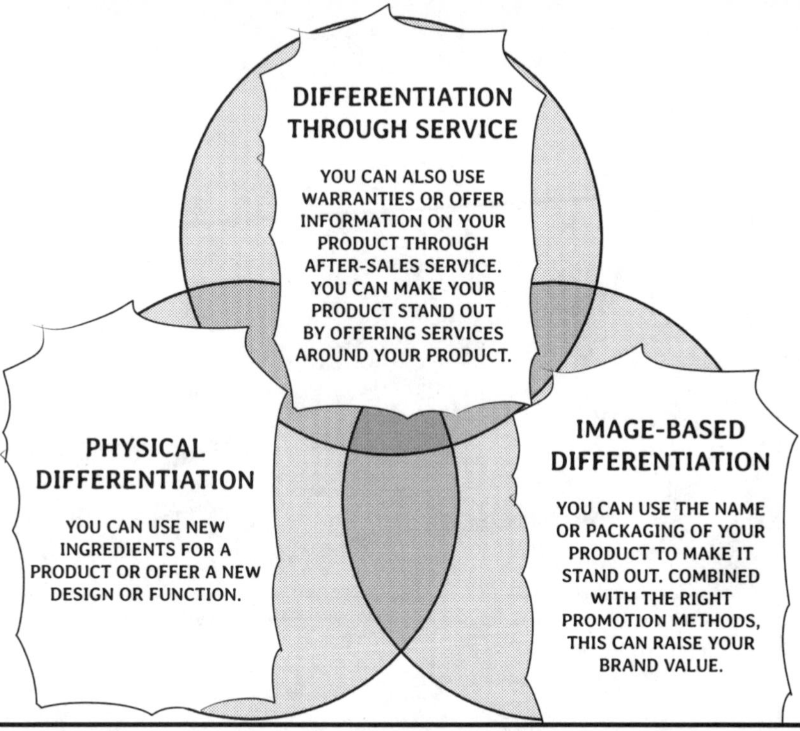
DIFFERENTIATION THROUGH SERVICE
YOU CAN ALSO USE WARRANTIES OR OFFER INFORMATION ON YOUR PRODUCT THROUGH AFTER-SALES SERVICE. YOU CAN MAKE YOUR PRODUCT STAND OUT BY OFFERING SERVICES AROUND YOUR PRODUCT.
PHYSICAL DIFFERENTIATION
YOU CAN USE NEW INGREDIENTS FOR A PRODUCT OR OFFER A NEW DESIGN OR FUNCTION.
IMAGE-BASED DIFFERENTIATION
YOU CAN USE THE NAME OR PACKAGING OF YOUR PRODUCT TO MAKE IT STAND OUT. COMBINED WITH THE RIGHT PROMOTION METHODS, THIS CAN RAISE YOUR BRAND VALUE.

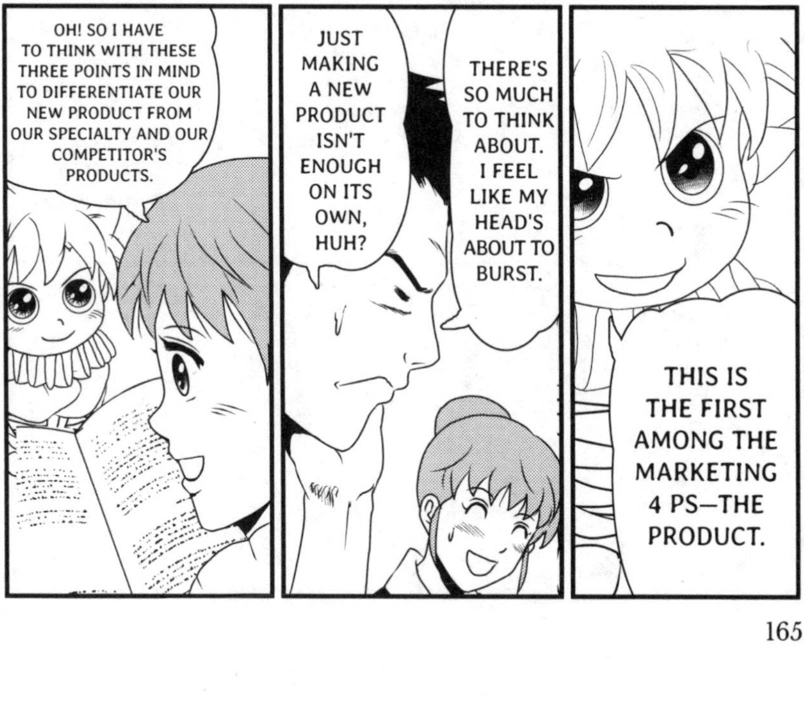
OH! SO I HAVE TO THINK WITH THESE THREE POINTS IN MIND TO DIFFERENTIATE OUR NEW PRODUCT FROM OUR SPECIALTY AND OUR COMPETITOR'S PRODUCTS.
JUST MAKING A NEW PRODUCT ISN'T ENOUGH ON ITS OWN, HUH?
THERE'S SO MUCH TO THINK ABOUT. I FEEL LIKE MY HEAD'S ABOUT TO BURST.
THIS IS THE FIRST AMONG THE MARKETING 4 PS—THE PRODUCT.

PROMOTION

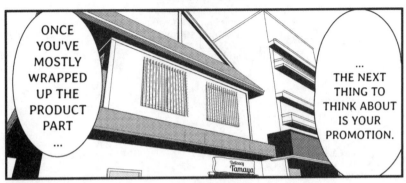

ONCE YOU'VE MOSTLY WRAPPED UP THE PRODUCT PART ...

... THE NEXT THING TO THINK ABOUT IS YOUR PROMOTION.

WE NEED TO BE CREATIVE TO LET PEOPLE KNOW ABOUT OUR PRODUCT AND MAKE THEM WANT TO BUY IT, RIGHT?

YUP.

THERE'S PULL MARKETING WHERE YOU TRY TO DRAW PEOPLE TO BUY YOUR PRODUCT BY TELLING THEM ABOUT IT.

ON THE OTHER HAND, YOU CAN ALSO DO PUSH MARKETING WHERE YOU AGGRESSIVELY CONVINCE YOUR CUSTOMERS TO BUY YOUR PRODUCT.

WE WANT MORE PEOPLE TO COME TO TAMAYA, SO I GUESS WE'LL HAVE TO THINK OF A PULL MARKETING STRATEGY.

YEAH ...

HMM? WHAT'S WRONG?

I WAS JUST THINKING THAT IT WOULD BE GREAT TO HAVE EMO AROUND FOR THIS.

I'M GOOD AT THINKING ABOUT THINGS LOGICALLY, WHILE EMO IS GOOD AT THINKING ABOUT PEOPLE'S EMOTIONS.

EMO'S ABILITIES ARE ESPECIALLY USEFUL FOR COMING UP WITH PROMOTIONAL PLANS.

COME TO THINK OF IT, I HAVEN'T SEEN HIM AT ALL SINCE THAT FIRST FAILED ATTEMPT.

WHERE COULD HE HAVE GONE? I HAVE NO HARD FEELINGS ABOUT IT...

EMO ...

... COME BACK.

Ta ma ya

WOULD YOU LIKE SOME TEA?

OH YEAH. WHEN WE WERE THINKING ABOUT THE PRODUCT EARLIER, THERE WAS AN IDEA WHERE WE MAKE IT LOOK LIKE WESTERN SWEETS INSTEAD OF TRADITIONAL JAPANESE ONES, RIGHT? DON'T YOU THINK THAT'S A TOPIC THAT'S EASY TO DISCUSS?

THAT MIGHT BE GOOD. MAYBE WE COULD HAVE THE MEDIA PICK UP THE TOPIC JUST LIKE EMO DID LAST TIME.

I GUESS THIS FALLS UNDER PROMOTION.

IF WE HAD MONEY, WE COULD PROBABLY RUN SOME ADVERTISING AS WELL, BUT THAT'D BE DIFFICULT RIGHT NOW. WE CAN PROBABLY MANAGE TO MAKE SOME SAMPLE PRODUCTS FOR SALES PROMOTIONS AT EVENTS AND STUFF.

!

THEN IT WOULD BE GOOD IF YOU HAD A STORY AROUND YOUR PRODUCT.

!

EMO!

IT'D PROBABLY BE NICE TO SHOW A SCENE OF A BIRTHDAY PARTY CELEBRATION WITH GRANDPARENTS TO CONVEY WHAT KIND OF THOUGHTS YOU HAD WHILE MAKING THE PRODUCT.

IF PEOPLE BUY YOUR PRODUCT AS A SUBSTITUTE FOR CAKES AT WEDDINGS OR BIRTHDAYS, IT COULD ALSO BE A CHANCE TO USE THE WORD-OF-MOUTH CHAIN.

EMO ...

MARIMO, LOGI, I...

EMO, RIGHT NOW, WE'RE TRYING TO DEVELOP A NEW PRODUCT TO CAPTURE A NEW PORTION OF CUSTOMERS. CAN YOU HELP US?

I THINK WE ALSO NEED TO THINK OF WAYS TO MOVE HUMAN EMOTIONS FOR THIS.

LOGI ...

RIGHT, MARIMO?

REALLY, WHERE HAVE YOU BEEN?!

YOU PROMISED TO HELP ME, DIDN'T YOU? COME ON IN ALREADY!

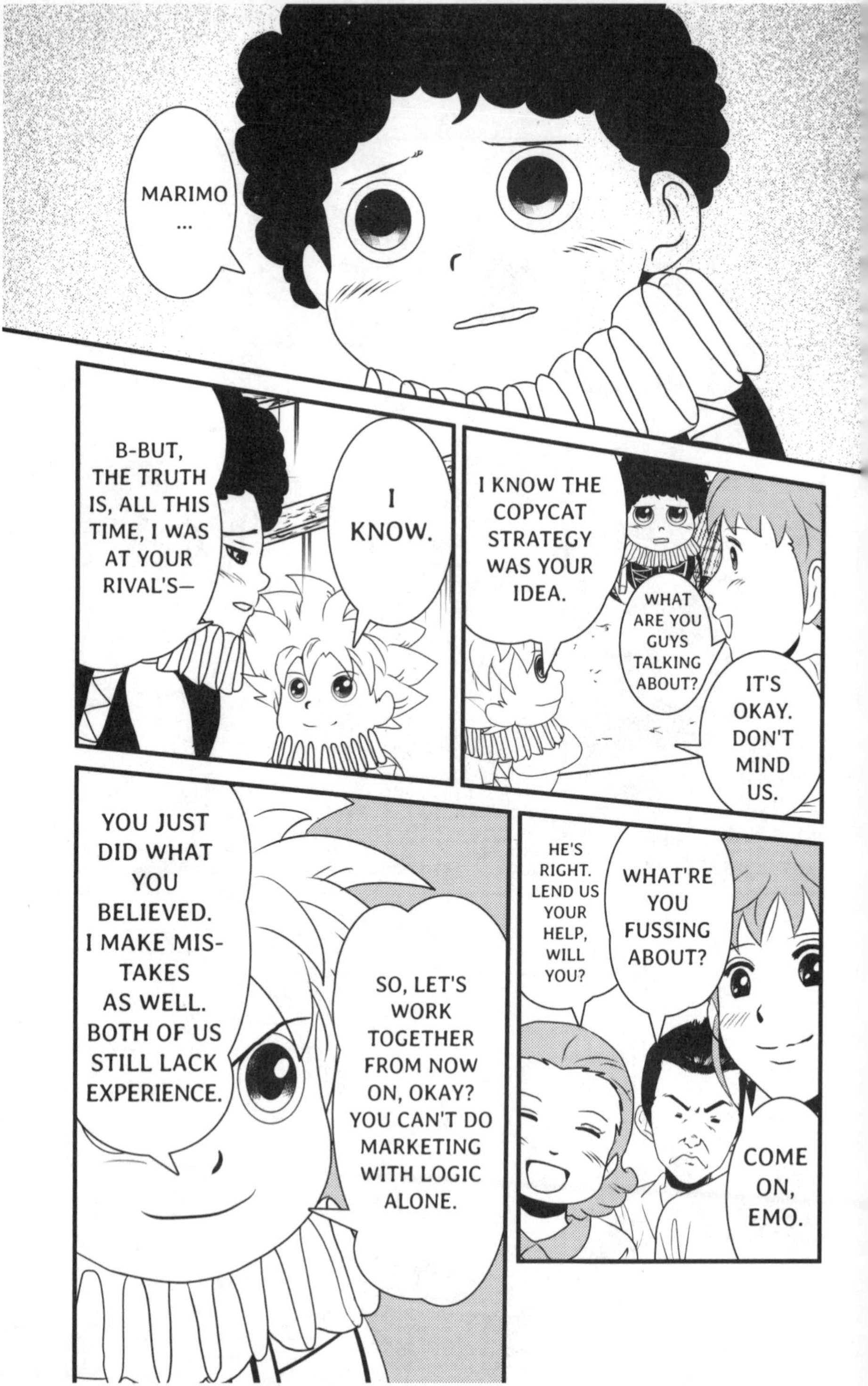
MARIMO ...
B-BUT, THE TRUTH IS, ALL THIS TIME, I WAS AT YOUR RIVAL'S—
I KNOW.
I KNOW THE COPYCAT STRATEGY WAS YOUR IDEA.
WHAT ARE YOU GUYS TALKING ABOUT?
IT'S OKAY. DON'T MIND US.
YOU JUST DID WHAT YOU BELIEVED. I MAKE MIS-TAKES AS WELL. BOTH OF US STILL LACK EXPERIENCE.
SO, LET'S WORK TOGETHER FROM NOW ON, OKAY? YOU CAN'T DO MARKETING WITH LOGIC ALONE.
HE'S RIGHT. LEND US YOUR HELP, WILL YOU?
WHAT'RE YOU FUSSING ABOUT?
COME ON, EMO.

THANK YOU.

Delicacy Tamaya

AT LAST, EMO AND LOGI ARE BACK TOGETHER.

NOW WE CAN CONTINUE TO DEVELOP OUR NEW PRODUCT TOGETHER!

PRICE

OKAY, I GET WHERE YOU'RE UP TO NOW. SO THE NEXT P OF THE 4 PS WE'LL TACKLE IS PRICE.

WHAT ARE YOU THINKING OF FOR THE PRICE?

HMM, FOR THE PRICE, LET'S GO WITH SOMETHING THAT EVEN KIDS CAN BUY. HOW ABOUT 500 YEN A BOX?

500 YEN ?!*

ISN'T THAT TOO SMALL TO COVER PRODUCTION COSTS?

THAT'S RIGHT. THE INGREDIENTS ALONE COST AROUND 1000 YEN. WE'LL BE OPERATING AT A LOSS.

BUT WHEN YOU LOOK AT THE PRICES AT SUPERMARKETS AND CONVENIENCE STORES—

THAT'S COMPETITOR-BASED PRICING. WHO ARE YOU EVEN COMPETING WITH? OF COURSE, YOU'LL BE IN THE RED WITH THAT.

BUT IF WE ALSO INCLUDE THE MANUFACTURING COST AND LABOR COST, THE PRICE WILL HAVE TO BE MORE THAN 2000 YEN.

NOW YOU'RE DOING COST-BASED PRICING.

■ PRICING POLICIES

Policy	Logic	Deciding Method	Other Names
Cost-based	Supplier logic (convenient for the company)	Adding a profit margin to the product cost and setting the price there	• Cost plus pricing • Profit-based pricing
Competition-based	Market logic (competitor-related)	Considering the product and its competition and trying to balance the price based on this	Competition-based value
Value-based	Demand logic (convenient for the consumer)	Studying in advance what the demand is at different prices and setting the product price based on the results	Competition-based value

---

*500 yen is approximately $4 USD

THINK, MARIMO!

YOUR PARENTS HAVE PROTECTED YOUR OLD AND TRADITIONAL IMAGE FOR SO LONG. WHAT WERE THEY TRYING TO PROTECT?

LOOKING AT THINGS BASED ON THIS BRAND, IT'S ONLY NATURAL THAT YOUR PRODUCTS ARE MORE EXPENSIVE THAN SUPERMARKET OR CONVENIENCE STORE MANJU.

PEOPLE WILL THINK OF A PRICE THAT FITS WITH A PLACE'S ATMOSPHERE AS THE RIGHT PRICE.

THIS IS THE PSYCHOLOGY OF PLACE. YOU'D DO WELL TO REMEMBER THAT.

PSYCHOLOGY OF PLACE

If you line up the same products at a convenience store and a luxury brand shop, people will feel that the products in the convenience store are cheaper while the products in the luxury brand shop are more expensive.

PRICE IS A COMPONENT OF BRAND VALUE

A higher price makes the brand feel more valuable.

THIS PRODUCT'S MAIN PURPOSE IS TO BRING NEW CUSTOMERS INTO THE STORE AND MAKE THEM LONG-TIME PATRONS. EVEN WITHOUT PROFIT, AS LONG AS THE COST OF INGREDIENTS AND OTHER EXPENSES ARE COVERED, IT SHOULD BE FINE. IT'S MORE EXPENSIVE THAN THE CONVENIENCE STORE MANJU, BUT WE'LL SET THE PRICE FOR THIS AT 1500 YEN.

LET'S GO WITH THIS PRICE!

PRICE

THE LAST OF THE 4 PS IS PLACE.

THIS IS WHERE YOU DECIDE WHAT ROUTE THE PRODUCT WILL TAKE TO REACH YOUR CUSTOMERS.

OF COURSE, THE MAIN ROUTE FOR US IS SELLING IT AT OUR STORE.

BESIDES THAT, WE COULD HAVE SOME STOCK SOLD IN LOCAL SOUVENIR SHOPS. WE COULD ALSO OFFER IT IN DEPARTMENT STORE EXHIBITS FROM TIME TO TIME.

THOSE ARE ALL IMPORTANT, BUT SINCE YOU'RE TRYING TO GET NEW CUSTOMERS, YOU ALSO NEED TO LOOK FOR A NEW SELLING OUTLET.

RIGHT.

THAT REMINDS ME. THE GRANDMA OF THE KIDS WHO CAME HERE BEFORE CALLED US TO ORDER SOME MANJU 'CAUSE SHE WANTED THEIR NEIGHBORS TO TASTE IT.

THAT'S IT.

YOU'LL HAVE TO FIND A WAY TO CAPTURE THOSE KINDS OF CUSTOMERS.

IF THAT'S THE CASE, YOU MAY WANT TO BE ABLE TO FULFILL MAIL ORDERS.

IF IT'S FOR SENIORS, THEN WE PROBABLY WANT TO ACCOMMODATE PHONE CALLS FIRST.

THAT'S NOT ENOUGH.

TO CAPTURE YOUNGER CUSTOMERS, YOU'LL ALSO WANT TO USE THE INTERNET.

SINCE YOU'RE ALREADY USING THE INTERNET, YOU SHOULD JUST OPEN AN INTERNET SHOP INSTEAD OF SIMPLY TAKING ORDERS.

GOOD IDEA, EMO!

YOU CAN THINK OF THE INTERNET AS ANOTHER SHOP, SO YOU MIGHT NEED A SEPARATE STORE MANAGER FOR THAT.

IF YOU'RE SELLING OVER THE INTERNET, YOU'D WANT TO MAKE GOOD USE OF INFORMATION YOU CAN GET ON SOCIAL NETWORKS, REVIEWS, AND REVIEW WEBSITES.

THAT'S THE FIRST THING I LEARNED!

RIGHT. YOU NEED TO WORK ON HUMAN EMOTIONS AND SUPPORT THEM. YOU NEED TO THINK OF A SYSTEM THAT SATISFIES YOUR CUSTOMERS.

THAT'S RIGHT.

EACH OF US ALONE ISN'T ENOUGH.

LOGIC AND EMOTION— YOU HAVE TO COMBINE AND CONSIDER BOTH.

HUH?! HEY, YOU GUYS. WHAT'S HAPPENING?

GLOW

SHINE

!

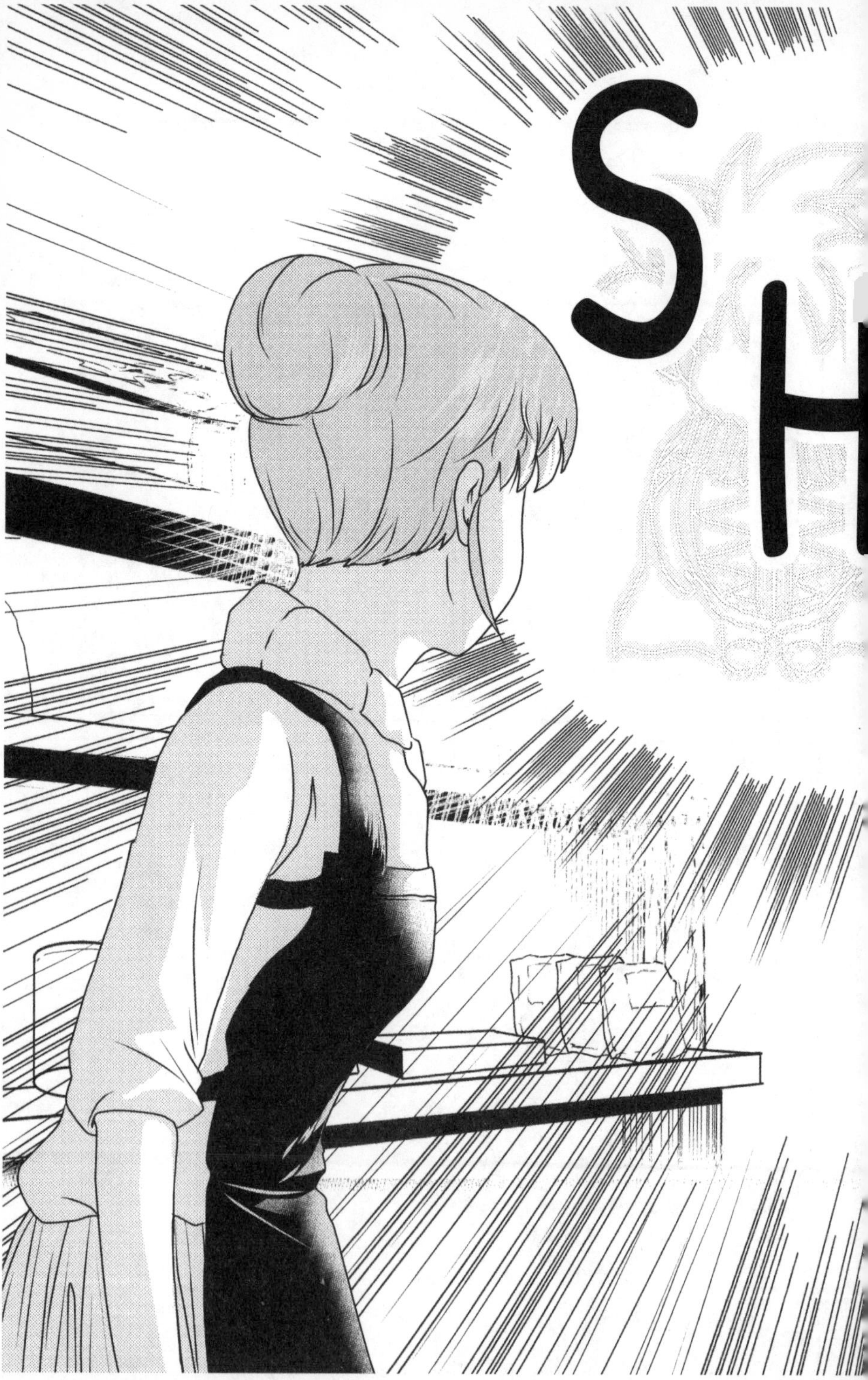
SH

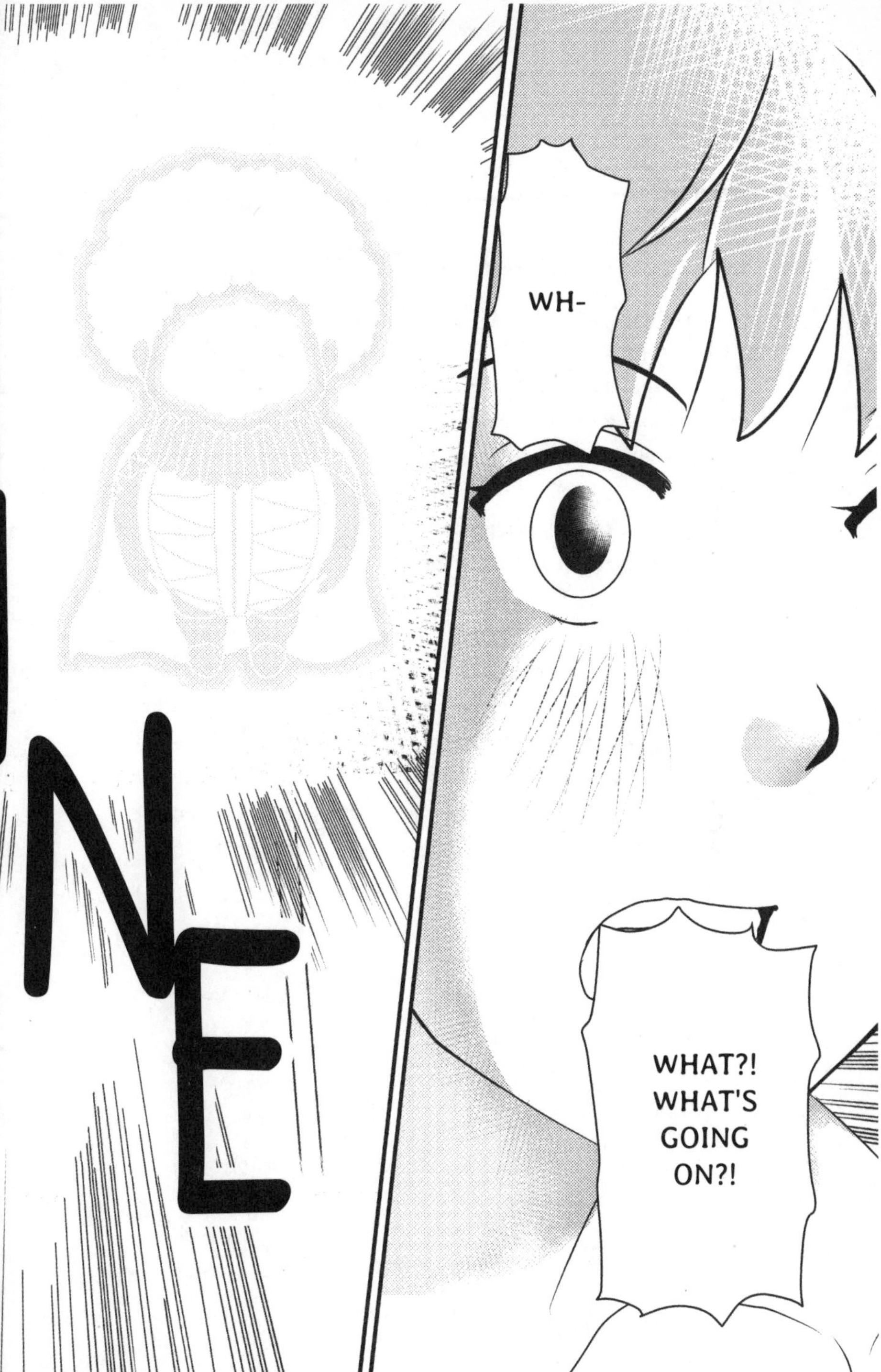
WH-
WHAT?! WHAT'S GOING ON?!
NE

What Are the 4 Ps of Marketing?

The 4 Ps that Logi talked about in the manga are **product, price, place,** and **promotion**. They make up the **marketing mix**. These components make up the details that you need when building a new product. They include everything that the company proposes to consumers for their new product.

Making the appropriate choices for each of the 4 Ps is important, but it's also necessary to make sure that the components are consistent with each other and work well together. For example, if you're offering consumable goods at a very low price, then it would be critical to make sure they are sold at supermarkets throughout the country and promoted through mass media like television. On the other hand, if you're trying to sell a branded product, you'll want to limit selling it in high-end places to protect your brand image and you'll want to set the price high. The idea is to make each of the 4 Ps work together to make each other more effective.

The 4 Ps of Marketing

Product	Price
Quality, type of product, design, unique features, brand name, packaging, size, service, warranty, product returns	Target price, discounts, golden handcuffs, payment period, credit terms
Place	**Promotion**
Channel, transport, inventory, scope of circulation, location, lineup	Communication mix (sales, advertising, and promotion), sales staff, direct marketing, online marketing

THERE ARE 4 PS FOR SELLERS. THEN THERE ARE 4 CS FOR BUYERS. WHEN SEEN FROM THE CUSTOMER'S POINT OF VIEW, PRODUCT CORRESPONDS TO CUSTOMER VALUE, PRICE TO COST, PLACE TO CONVENIENCE, AND PROMOTION TO COMMUNICATION.

Key Points for Differentiating Between Products

The first of the 4 Ps is **product**. In the story, Logi explained that when developing a new product or service, there are three points you want to keep in mind when differentiating your product: (1) physical differentiation, (2) image-based differentiation, and (3) service differentiation.

For **physical differentiation**, you can use new ingredients for a product or offer a new design or function that's never been offered before.

For **image-based differentiation**, you can use the name or packaging of your product and combine it with the right promotional methods to raise your brand value or push a specific image that customers can associate with your product.

In **service differentiation**, you can offer warranties, information on your product through after-sales service, and various other services around your product to differentiate yourself from competitors.

Marimo and her family made many different variations of manju with unique ingredients. They then picked the best from those flavors and made smaller versions to sell as a set. They also came up with the idea of offering the set in a gift box to introduce other use cases. They combined various physical and image-based things to make the product stand out. Differentiating your new product from your existing ones and competitors opens the possibility of grabbing the interest of both new customers and the media. There's a wide range of things you can pack in the product component of marketing, and the combination of each of these becomes important in building the whole.

With more advanced manufacturing technology and the quick spread of information over the Internet today, you will see similar products pop up one after another within a short period. As such, it becomes important to keep on formulating strategies to continuously differentiate your product from others.

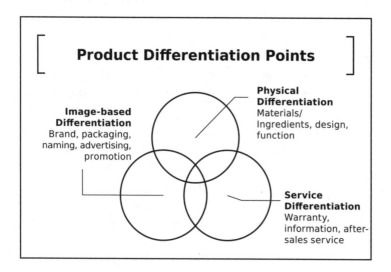

Product Differentiation Points

Image-based Differentiation
Brand, packaging, naming, advertising, promotion

Physical Differentiation
Materials/Ingredients, design, function

Service Differentiation
Warranty, information, after-sales service

What Is a Brand?

One of the most important things in differentiating a product is having a **brand**. This term is now casually used in our conversations all the time, so it might be a little harder to define what it actually is. Let's try looking more closely at what makes up a brand.

At the beginning of the manga in Part 4, one of Tamaya's regular customer talks to Marimo about seeing their products in supermarkets and convenience stores. Tamaya's special manju exists in that customer's mind as a brand, and when she saw a product similar to that manju, she automatically thought it was Tamaya's. Consumers knowing your brand name and symbol this way is termed **brand recognition**, while associating certain ideas and images with a brand is termed **brand association**. Having a wide range of consumers share a common brand recognition and brand association knowledge is what makes up a brand. You have successfully established your brand when people have an idea of what kind of store you have, what kind of products or services you offer, and the expected corresponding price range just from seeing your brand name or symbol. You can see how big a brand is by the number of people who share the same ideas about it.

What Is a Brand?

Knowledge about a brand grows into memories in the mind of consumers.

Brand Recognition
Recognizing a brand name or symbol

- "Oh, the traditional delicacy shop, Tamaya!"

Brand Association
Things that people associate with your brand

- "Marimo Manju!"
- "They have a traditional image."
- "Their matcha tastes great!"

How Do You Build Your Brand?

Various components lead to brand recognition and association. Your **brand name** is the concise expression of the concept of your brand and is very much connected with recognition and association. The **logo mark** is a visual representation of your company name or service name and serves to distinguish your product or service from others. A **character** is a visual representation of the personality of your brand and is used when you want to build a friendlier brand.

Other important components of your brand include the **slogan**, which is a descriptive and persuasive concise phrase about your brand. There's also the **jingle**, which is a message about your brand in musical form. Your **packaging** is the container that protects your product from damage while also functioning as a form of advertising.

To establish the brand of their newly developed product, Marimo and her family will have to think carefully about each of these components. They'll have to think of a name that will match the actual product and choose typesetting and visuals that represent that name. They'll have to decide on all these different components and make sure that they balance out nicely with each other.

What Makes up a Brand?

Component	Description
Brand Name	Concisely expresses the concept of your brand. Points to consider are how easy it is to remember, how well it conveys meaning, and how good it sounds.
Logo Mark	A visual representation of the company name or service name that distinguishes your product from others. Functions to guarantee the quality, declare the manufacturer, or work as a form of advertising.
Character	A visual representation of your brand's personality. Used when you want a friendly brand.
Slogan	A descriptive and persuasive concise phrase about the brand.
Jingle	A combination of music and sounds conveying a musical message regarding the brand. Works well in raising brand recognition.
Packaging	The design and creation of a product's container and wrapping. Aside from protecting the product from damage, it makes transport and storage more convenient and helps in advertising and promotion.

5

The Product Life Cycle

Products follow a cycle from birth to decline. This is called the **product life cycle**. In the graph on the next page, time is represented on the horizontal axis and the value of sales and profit is represented on the vertical. More time has passed the farther you go to the right on the horizontal axis. At the leftmost of the time axis is when the product is born. As you move farther to the right, the product goes through its introduction, growth, maturity, and decline phases—just like a human going through life.

Let's look at the characteristics of each period. During the **introduction** stage, the majority of your customers are innovators. Sales are low and you hardly have any profit.

In the **growth** stage, your competitors enter the market, but as the market itself is expanding, you experience big sales and high profits.

Once you're past the sales peak and you enter the **maturity** stage, the competition between rivals gets tough. You often compete on prices, and so your profits decrease.

Finally, you'll enter the **decline** stage, and both your sales and profits steadily decline.

By constantly being aware of what product life cycle stage your product is currently in, you can correctly determine what marketing measures you need and pick the right timing to introduce improvements to your product as you consider its future.

In the case of Tamaya, their specialty has already had a very long life cycle. From the decrease in customers, you can tell that the product is already past its maturity stage. To maintain the status of its specialty products, Tamaya will have to make adjustments to its

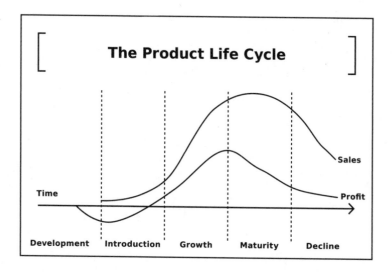

ingredients, size, and other product components. The changes will have to be practically unnoticeable to most customers while still matching their changing needs. At the same time, Marimo and her family can extend the life cycle of their new product by offering flavors that match the season or by adding some time-limited flavors.

You can observe this pattern with various big burger chains and snack manufacturers that have a large number of repeat customers. You'll find that they keep putting in this steady effort to keep their products popular.

By understanding the product life cycle, you will be able to think of the necessary product development measures at the right time and apply them as appropriate to your product.

Unique Characteristics at Different Stages of the Product Life Cycle

	Introduction	Growth	Maturity	Decline
• Characteristics				
Sales	Low	Rapid growth	Slow growth	Decline
Profit	Almost none or negative	Reaches peak	A steady decline from peak	Very low
Main Customers	Innovators, early adopters	Early majority, late majority	Late majority	Late majority
Competitors	Almost none	Increasing	Many	Decline
• Strategies to Take				
Strategy Focus	Market expansion	Market penetration	Maintaining market share	Manufacturing efficiency
Circulation Channels	Undeveloped	Expansion/ maintenance	Choose main channels	Choose and limit channels
Promotion Focus	Increase recognition	Establish brand	Maintain loyalty	Selective
Price	High	A bit low	Even lower	Raise prices

6

Push and Pull Marketing Strategies

The second of the 4 Ps is **promotion.** Promotional activities involve both pull and push marketing.

Pull marketing aims to attract customers to your product. This involves assertively promoting your product's appeal through television, newspapers, and magazines. You lead people to become interested in your product and to take action to buy it themselves. If your product is the type that a lot of consumers want, retail stores will try to stock up on more and be bullish in placing orders with you.

On the other hand, **push marketing** involves aggressive sales promotion to push customers to buy your product. The manufacturer will usually dispatch a salesperson to the retail store, have display cabinets, make points of purchase specifically for promotion, prepare pamphlets, and offer samples. Since support from the manufacturer also makes it easier to sell products at the retail store, this assertive sales promotion works. Products are usually displayed in a prominent area in the store and are aggressively promoted to customers.

In most cases, companies will employ a combination of push and pull marketing.

Push and Pull Marketing

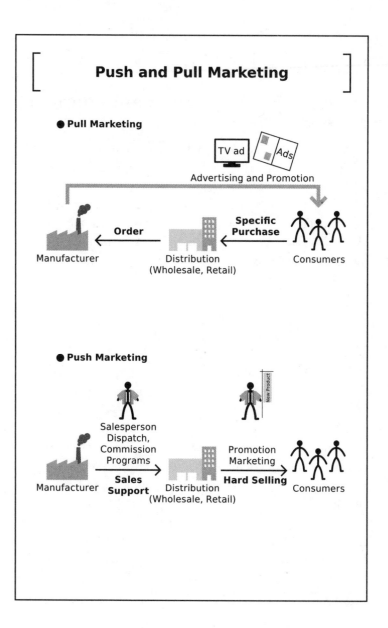

● **Pull Marketing**

TV ad Ads

Advertising and Promotion

Manufacturer ← **Order** ← Distribution (Wholesale, Retail) ← **Specific Purchase** ← Consumers

● **Push Marketing**

Salesperson Dispatch, Commission Programs

New Product

Manufacturer → **Sales Support** → Distribution (Wholesale, Retail) → Promotion Marketing / **Hard Selling** → Consumers

Different Promotional Communication Methods

There are many ways to spread information about your product. These range from television, newspaper, and outdoor advertisements to distributing fliers, sponsoring events, and sending your product to information programs on television. The combination of the different methods you use to spread information about your product is called the **communication mix (promotion mix)** and is comprised of the push and pull strategies explained on page 192.

Pull-type promotions mostly involve having newspapers and magazines write articles about your product. You can pay to have ads in newspapers and magazines or use fliers. Sales promotion involves offering samples, holding events, and sponsoring other activities that involve direct communication with consumers.

Push-type promotions are quite similar to pull-type sales promotions. They involve catching people's attention with large exhibitions where customers can directly buy your product as well as directly convincing customers to buy your product at retail stores.

Face-to-face selling is yet another promotional communication technique that involves having salespersons and sales staff directly trying to sell your products to customers.

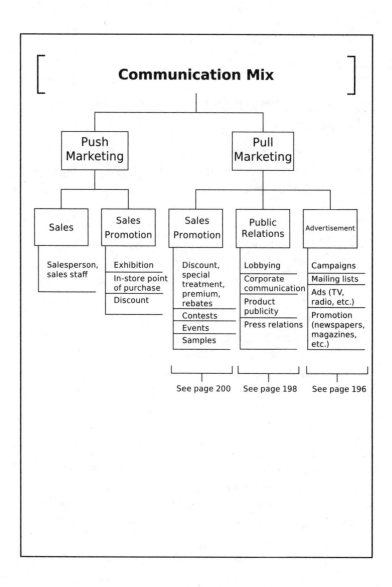

Communication Mix

Push Marketing		Pull Marketing		
Sales	Sales Promotion	Sales Promotion	Public Relations	Advertisement
Salesperson, sales staff	Exhibition	Discount, special treatment, premium, rebates	Lobbying	Campaigns
	In-store point of purchase	Contests	Corporate communication	Mailing lists
	Discount	Events	Product publicity	Ads (TV, radio, etc.)
		Samples	Press relations	Promotion (newspapers, magazines, etc.)

See page 200   See page 198   See page 196

8

The Features of Different Advertising Methods

Advertising continues to expand and evolve with the changing times. It used to be focused mainly on the four types of mass media: television, radio, newspaper, and magazines.

Television ads offer the advantage of repetition and are able to reach a wide audience so they are good for letting a lot of people know about your product at once. But television ads are expensive and not always feasible for small businesses. Radio ads are relatively cheaper but tend to have a more limited audience. Newspaper media offer the advantage of being able to target a specific audience with specialist newspapers. They have high credibility, which makes it easier for customers to trust your product. If there is a specialist magazine related to your product, magazines can let you target very specific segments while keeping your costs down.

On the Internet, search keywords and browsing history can be used to display relevant ads to consumers. You can also have people introduce your product in their blogs or use social networks for guaranteed effective advertising. Internet advertising is continuously evolving every day and currently ranks close to television ads in increasing product sales.

For outdoor advertising, billboards were once the main method of promoting products, but today you can find ads on buses, train cars, train station floors, and ticket gates.

	The Four Mass Media				Internet	Outdoor Ads
	TV	Radio	Newspaper	Magazine		
Contact Time	Short	Short	Depends on interest	Depends on interest	Depends on interest	Short
Explanatory Ability	Low	Low	High	High	High	Very low
Repetition	Raising this will increase the cost	Raising this will increase the cost	Low	Low	Raising this will increase the cost	Expensive for certain types
Area	Cannot target a specific area	Cannot target a specific area	Can target a specific area	Mixed	Essentially global	Limited
Segment	Depends on time slot	Depends on time slot	Can target a specific segment for specialized papers	Can target a specific segment	Can target through keywords	Depends on location
Advantage	A high number of impressions	Relatively cheaper	Credibility	Can target a specific audience	Interactive	Low cost

The Effects of Public Relations

In addition to advertising and sales promotion, an important component of the communication mix is **public relations (PR)**. PR involves offering information about your company and product to the mass media and having them report about it in the form of news or information. Since this is taken as objective information, it can more easily lead to higher sales. However, the disadvantage of PR is that, unlike advertising, you cannot control what information about your product gets reported.

Regardless of company size, it is common practice to make use of press releases to introduce a new product or service by sending information about it to different news outlets. You can also hold press conferences and interviews to relay information. If a product or service has a high social value or is newsworthy, there's a possibility that the media will cover it as news.

In the manga, Emo suggests telling their new product's development story or showing scenes of it being used to catch the attention of the media. If you are able to convey what's interesting about your product, it's possible to attract more customers without spending a lot of money on promotion.

The Difference between Advertising and Public Relations

	Advertising	Public Relations
Credibility to consumers	Tends to have a reputation for saying only good things for promotion	Tends to be taken as objective information from the media
Information content	Focused on product information	Includes personnel and management information
Certainty of information transmission	Can be controlled. If paid for, transmission is certain	Cannot be controlled. Everything from content to publication is controlled by the media
Publication form	Advertisements	Articles and information
Exposure	Limited to the advertising slot secured	Can develop in various ways depending on the content
Cost	High cost; includes production costs and advertising fees	Costs little when done well; limited labor and communication expenses
Strategic role	Presents an answer	Presents a question

Various Sales Promotion Methods

Sales promotion involves direct promotion to consumers, such as offering product samples, holding events, and promoting discounts at storefronts. While advertising and PR are indirect methods that try to convey a product's appeal, sales promotion tries to directly convince consumers to purchase a product.

It's important to formulate an effective communication mix by combining different types of sales promotion with your advertising and PR. Promotional events designed to raise the image of a product include cultural events like concerts or art exhibits or sporting events like football and baseball.

Contests can raise awareness and interest in your products. For example, you could hold a popularity contest for recipes that use specific ingredients like your product.

You can also raise your sales by giving your customers the satisfaction of a bargain through discounts, premiums, and rebates.

Common Sales Promotion Methods (Classified According to Type)

Type		Description
Event	Cultural/ sports events	Aims to improve product image through sports and cultural events
	Sales promotion event	Aims for on-site purchases like product exhibits, etc.
	Hybrid events	Combines on-site selling with sports/ cultural events
Contest	Usage contest	Contests that involve different ways of using a product
	Writing contest	Contests for writing articles or essays on a certain theme
	Popularity contest	Popularity contests that aim to shape the image of the superiority of a product or service
Discount, special treatment	Coupon	Discount coupons or complimentary tickets for a product or service; also includes Internet and store coupons
	Voucher	Vouchers you can exchange for a certain product or service
Premiums (extras, prizes)	Freebies as prizes	Can give prizes directly in exchange for collecting stamps or stickers or through raffle entries
	Freebies as gifts	Can come inside the product package, outside the product package, separately packed, or as bonus contents in the same package
Rebates	Cash back	Can come with a product purchase, as stickers to collect with each purchase, or by collecting points from each purchase. Points can be used for discounts or can be used for payment instead of cash.

Three Ways to Decide on Your Prices

The question of what price to charge for a product isn't an easy thing to decide. Just like Marimo, you can decide a price based on the prices of competitors, but you can also decide a product's price based on its total cost. This is a problem that always has the people in charge racking their brains to make a decision. Let's try looking at three basic pricing policies: (1) cost-based pricing, (2) competition-based pricing, and (3) value-based pricing.

In **cost-based pricing**, the price is determined after adding what you think is an appropriate amount of profit to your product manufacturing cost. This method was once common when markets were seller-driven, but today it is too easy for rivals to compete based on price alone, so it is no longer commonly used.

With advancements in technology and sales networks, the difference between products has gotten smaller and smaller. Because of this, setting product prices through **competition-based pricing** has become more common at present. With this pricing method, you decide your product's price based on competitor prices. You gather products that are similar to yours and check their prices, then set your product's price at a similar point. This is the simplest pricing policy and the one with the least probability of failure.

In **value-based pricing**, the price is determined based on product demand. In the case of completely new products, research is conducted in advance to forecast how much demand there would be at different prices. The price is then decided based on that.

Pricing Policy Patterns

Policy	Logic	Deciding Method	Other Names
Cost-based	Supplier logic (convenient for the company)	Adding a profit margin to the product cost and setting the price there	• Cost plus pricing • Profit-based pricing
Competition-based	Market logic (competitor-related)	Considering the product and its competition and trying to balance the price based on this	Competition-based value
Value-based	Demand logic (convenient for the consumer)	Studying in advance what the demand is at different prices and setting the product price based on the results	Competition-based value

Determining Prices Based on Demand

One of the analyses used for value-based pricing is the **profit split method (PSM)** (see the chart on the next page). In this method, consumers are asked four questions. By compiling and plotting the results on a graph, you can determine what the ideal price is for most consumers. By relating these results to product quality, you can decide on a price that's based on statistics.

In the graph on the next page, on the vertical axis, you have the percentage of respondents with a maximum of 100%, and on the horizontal axis, you have the price which increases as you go farther to the right. By plotting the answers for all four questions on the graph, you will get four intersection points.

From the results, you can determine various price points. The "highest price" gives the most profit and is ideal for luxury items. The "lowest price at which quality is assured" is ideal for mass-market products where you want sales to be as high as possible. The middle-ground price is the price that people think of as "just okay." At the "ideal price," you can maintain a certain level of profit while also having relatively high sales from your product.

PSM Analysis

- The Four Questions for PSM Analysis

  Question 1
  At what price do you start to feel like this product is too expensive?

  Question 2
  At what price do you start to feel like this product is too cheap?

  Question 3
  At what price do you feel like this product is too expensive to buy?

  Question 4
  At what price do you feel like this product is too cheap and start doubting its quality?

- PSM Analysis Results

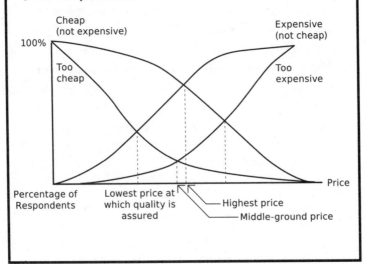

The Psychology of Prices and Pricing

Many factors affect a product's perceived value. Aside from the product's function and performance, its value is affected by its image and even by the atmosphere of the place where it's sold. Whenever we buy products, we unconsciously evaluate and judge them on the whole based on all these factors.

An example is the psychology of place that Logi explained in the manga. Consumers restrain themselves or let themselves loose based on their image of the place they are in. Aside from a select few, convenience stores normally don't offer products that go above ten dollars or so. This is because consumers normally won't go to convenience stores to buy expensive products. On the other hand, department stores offer many products that sell at the order of hundreds of dollars. This is because most people don't feel any resistance to spending this kind of money at department stores. **The amount that people perceive as okay to spend changes for different places.**

This aspect of human psychology is mysterious, and even small tricks in pricing can move people's hearts. A list of common pricing tricks is compiled on the next page.

The Psychology of Prices and Pricing

	Description
Psychology of Place	Depending on the state or atmosphere of the place, the amount of money that people think is okay to spend changes.
Value of Brand	The amount of money people are willing to spend on a product becomes higher with brand names or logos even if the products have the same quality.
Value of Reputation	For products that show social status like gems, art, and branded products, raising the price also raises the perceived quality.
Charm Pricing	People will perceive a price as lower when set at prices just below a round number like 99 cents or $9.99.
Exact Pricing	Setting the price at a round number makes it easier for customers to calculate their total spending, and they can pick and buy products worry-free.
"Frequently Bought Together" Suggestions	Suggesting other products around an expensive purchase makes customers feel like they just bought them with the main purchase and gives the impression of a bargain.
Psychological Wallet	This is the tendency of people to have separate psychological wallets for luxury and everyday goods so that they would spare no expense for expensive luxury goods but still hesitate when buying relatively cheaper everyday goods.

Think about How to Distribute Your Products

Last but not least among the 4 Ps is **place**. Place includes anything that has to do with where you sell your product to consumers—from distribution channels to retail stores.

Luxury brands, daily necessities that everyone needs, and products made with specific hobbyists in mind—different types of products have different characteristics, and the places where you can and should sell them will be different. Because of this, it's important to formulate your distribution strategy by deciding what route to take and what target segment you'll be offering your product to.

The route your product takes is its distribution channel, and there are multiple types. In the manga, Marimo and the others talked about orders by mail, telephone, and Internet. These methods fall under direct distribution. In **direct distribution**, you directly send your product to your customers by using mail and other shipping services.

Indirect distribution involves selling your product in existing physical retail stores. You can opt for open distribution like Kiza Bakery did when they sold their products at various retailers like supermarkets and convenience stores, or you can opt for closed distribution like Tamaya did when they sold their products only at limited retailers.

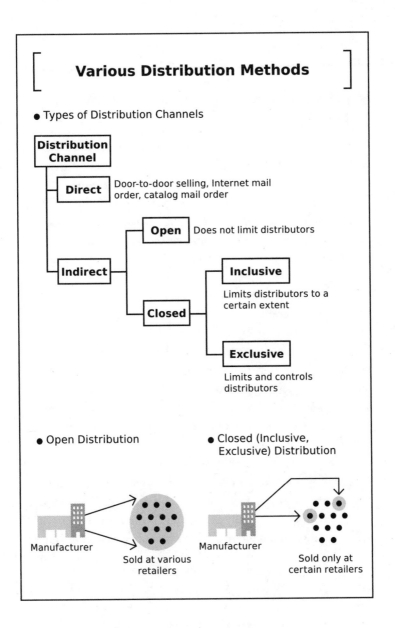

Various Distribution Methods

● Types of Distribution Channels

Distribution Channel

— **Direct** — Door-to-door selling, Internet mail order, catalog mail order

— **Indirect**

Open — Does not limit distributors

Closed

Inclusive

Limits distributors to a certain extent

Exclusive

Limits and controls distributors

● Open Distribution

● Closed (Inclusive, Exclusive) Distribution

Manufacturer

Sold at various retailers

Manufacturer

Sold only at certain retailers

Finding the Special Features of Your Market Area

The entire zone covered by the areas of residence of all consumers who can potentially visit your store is called your **market area**. This is the area from which you can gather your customers. The simplest way to determine your market area is to measure a certain radius around your shop. If you want to establish a more accurate area, you will have to look into how far the highways are and the travel time to and from your shop.

Whether or not you've already built your shop, it's very important to know the different characteristics of your market area. If you don't know these characteristics, you cannot convince potential customers to visit your shop. By knowing the market area population, characteristics of the residents, and consumption habits in the area, you can look into how many people live in the area and what kind of products they tend to want. Based on this, you can think of what kind of product the consumers would likely be happy to buy from you.

Of course, you will have multiple competitors within the same market area, and it will be important to look into them. By visiting these competitors, you can compare and contrast them with your store and think of ways to make more customers visit your store.

Points Related to Your Market Area

	Description
Market Area Population	An indicator used to measure the latent potential of a market area; determined by collecting demographics like gender, age, number of households, etc.
Population Characteristics	Describes the population's lifestyle and awareness by collecting information on business composition, private vehicle ownership, residence type, household composition, income level, etc.
Natural Characteristics of the Area	Used to understand the population's way of life by looking into the region's history, culture, climate, lifestyle, etc.
Consumption Trends	Describes the region's consumption habits by looking into actual statistics like consumer spending data
Access to Your Shop	By studying the access routes to your shop, you can check and remove obstacles that limit access like unclear signs, and you can also take measures to deal with possible needs like bicycle parking.
Competitor Shops	Studies competitors by actually looking into their product categorization, the number of customers who visit their shop, their customer conversion rate, their bestsellers, their price range, their display and selling area, etc.

The Functions of Wholesale

Wholesalers are companies that buy products from various manufacturers and distribute these products to various retailers. Dealing with a single wholesaler lets manufacturers sell their products at various retailers, making it possible for retailers to have stocks of various products from different manufacturers.

To cut distribution costs, it's recently becoming more popular for manufacturers to deal directly with retailers. To resist this change, the wholesale business has been strengthening its various functions.

One of the functions they cover is **information transfer**. They provide information on best-selling products to the manufacturers, and they provide the retailers with information related to sales promotion like information on new products or product features. They can fulfill this role because they have access to various information from various manufacturers and retailers. They also provide logistics by offering warehousing for manufacturers and transporting their products to retailers as needed. Wholesalers are indispensable for small manufacturers who will find it difficult to strike deals with big retailers.

Wholesalers also function as bearers of financial risk by stabilizing the cash flow for manufacturers and retailers as they wait until their products are sold.

The Role and Functions of Wholesale

● **Wholesalers**

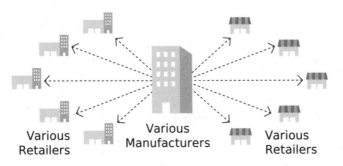

Various
Retailers

Various
Manufacturers

Various
Retailers

● **The Functions of Wholesale**

Function	Description
Information Transfer	Offers manufacturers useful information for product development and offers retailers useful information for sales promotion
Logistics	Takes care of warehousing for manufacturers who need it and transports products to retailers as needed
Wholesale Supplier	To limit the number of companies they have to deal with, retailers buy a wide range of products from a single wholesaler
Bearing Financial Risk	Stabilizes cash flow for manufacturers and retailers

Organizing and Preparing Your Present Product Strategy

Product portfolio management (PPM) organizes information about your products into a matrix. The market growth rate is an indicator related to the product life cycle while the relative market share is an indicator that shows the degree to which the experience curve effect (as production increases, production cost decreases) has affected your production.

Placing your company's ventures and products into this matrix should help you see and think of what steps you need to take for each of these ventures and products.

PPM organizes your products into Question Marks, Stars, Cash Cows, and Dogs. Companies will try to make as many Cash Cows as they can since these products contribute a lot to their profit. They will then invest those profits into the Question Marks in order to create new sources of revenue. Companies are able to aim for long-term growth by going through this cycle.

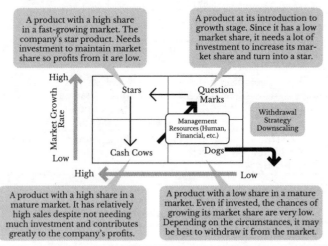

A product with a high share in a fast-growing market. The company's star product. Needs investment to maintain market share so profits from it are low.

A product at its introduction to growth stage. Since it has a low market share, it needs a lot of investment to increase its market share and turn into a star.

A product with a high share in a mature market. It has relatively high sales despite not needing much investment and contributes greatly to the company's profits.

A product with a low share in a mature market. Even if invested, the chances of growing its market share are very low. Depending on the circumstances, it may be best to withdraw it from the market.

Part 7

Establishing Long-Term Relationships with Your Customers

LOGI?

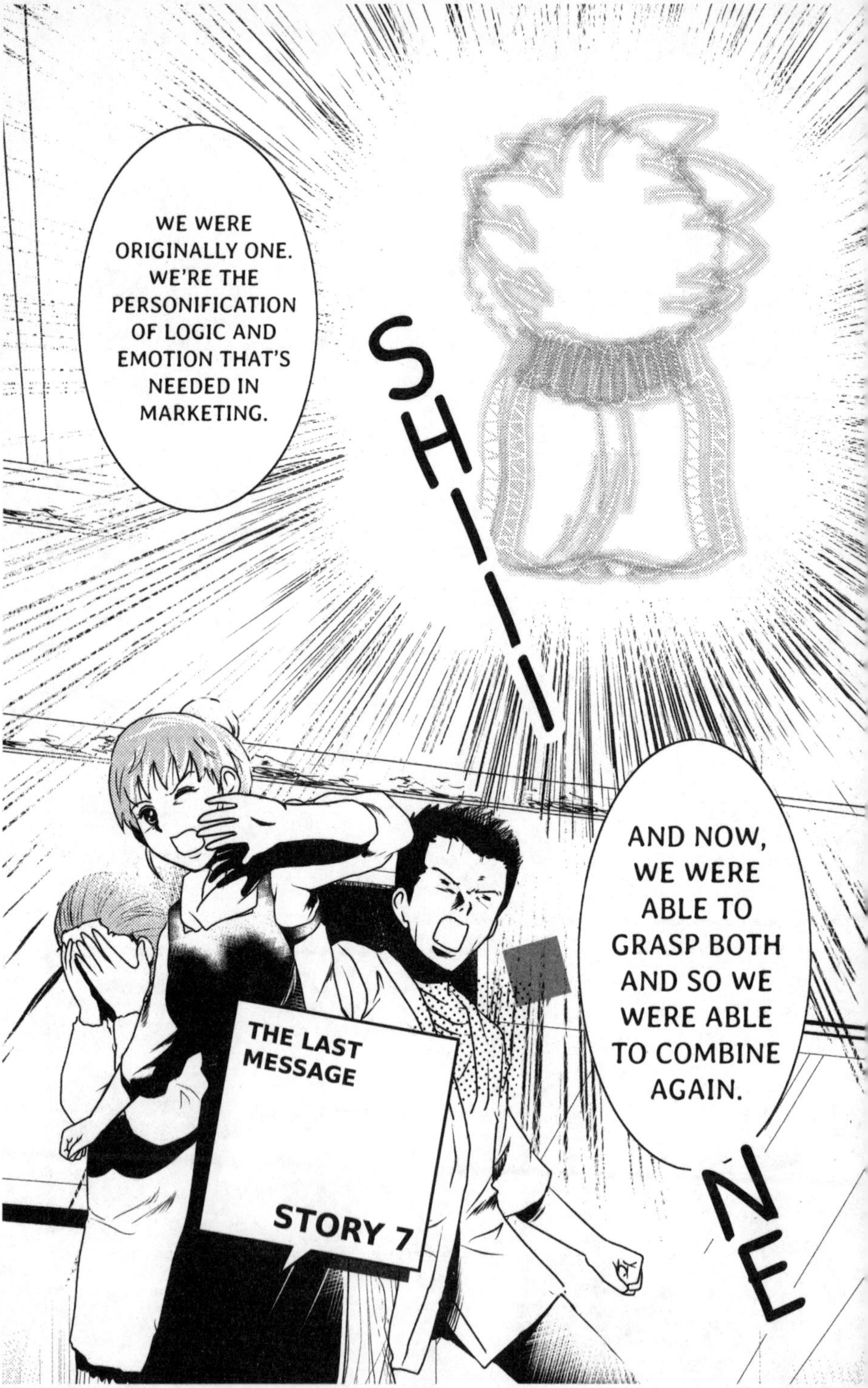
WE WERE ORIGINALLY ONE. WE'RE THE PERSONIFICATION OF LOGIC AND EMOTION THAT'S NEEDED IN MARKETING.
SHI—NE
AND NOW, WE WERE ABLE TO GRASP BOTH AND SO WE WERE ABLE TO COMBINE AGAIN.
THE LAST MESSAGE
STORY 7

MARIMO, IT SEEMS OUR JOB HERE IS DONE.

WHAT ?!

YOU'VE WORKED REALLY HARD.

THANKS TO YOU, WE WERE ABLE TO BECOME ONE AGAIN AND NOW WE WILL BE RETURNING TO HEAVEN SHORTLY.

NO WAY! WHAT ARE YOU SAYING?! YOU NEED TO HELP ME MORE!

IT'LL BE FINE. JUST AS WE ARE NOW ABLE TO BECOME ONE, THESE TWO VIEWPOINTS SHOULD'VE ALSO BEEN BORN INSIDE YOU. YOU WON'T MAKE THE SAME MISTAKES AS BEFORE.

WE HAVE A FINAL LESSON FOR YOU.

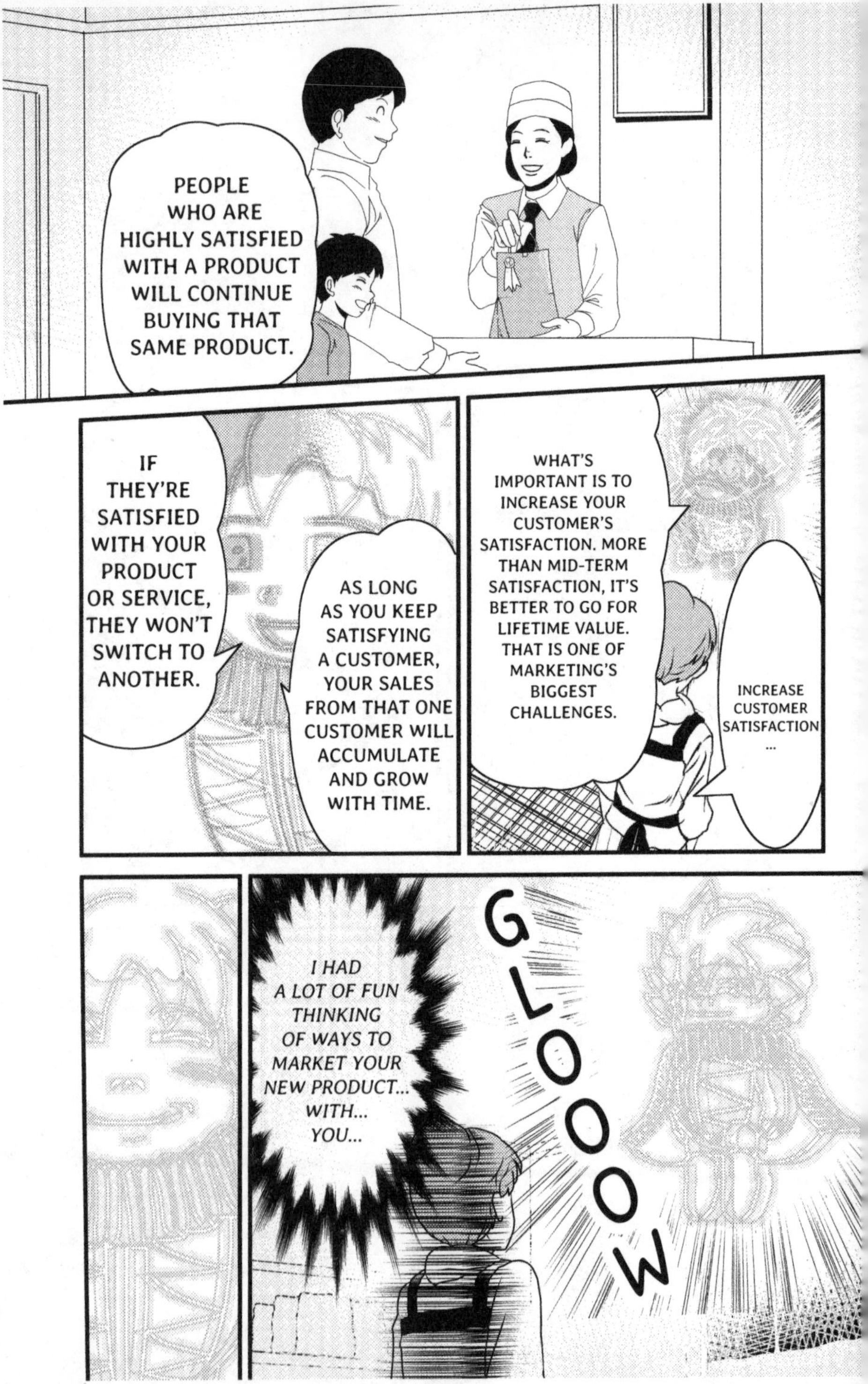
PEOPLE WHO ARE HIGHLY SATISFIED WITH A PRODUCT WILL CONTINUE BUYING THAT SAME PRODUCT.
WHAT'S IMPORTANT IS TO INCREASE YOUR CUSTOMER'S SATISFACTION. MORE THAN MID-TERM SATISFACTION, IT'S BETTER TO GO FOR LIFETIME VALUE. THAT IS ONE OF MARKETING'S BIGGEST CHALLENGES.
INCREASE CUSTOMER SATISFACTION ...
IF THEY'RE SATISFIED WITH YOUR PRODUCT OR SERVICE, THEY WON'T SWITCH TO ANOTHER.
AS LONG AS YOU KEEP SATISFYING A CUSTOMER, YOUR SALES FROM THAT ONE CUSTOMER WILL ACCUMULATE AND GROW WITH TIME.
GLOOOW
I HAD A LOT OF FUN THINKING OF WAYS TO MARKET YOUR NEW PRODUCT... WITH... YOU...

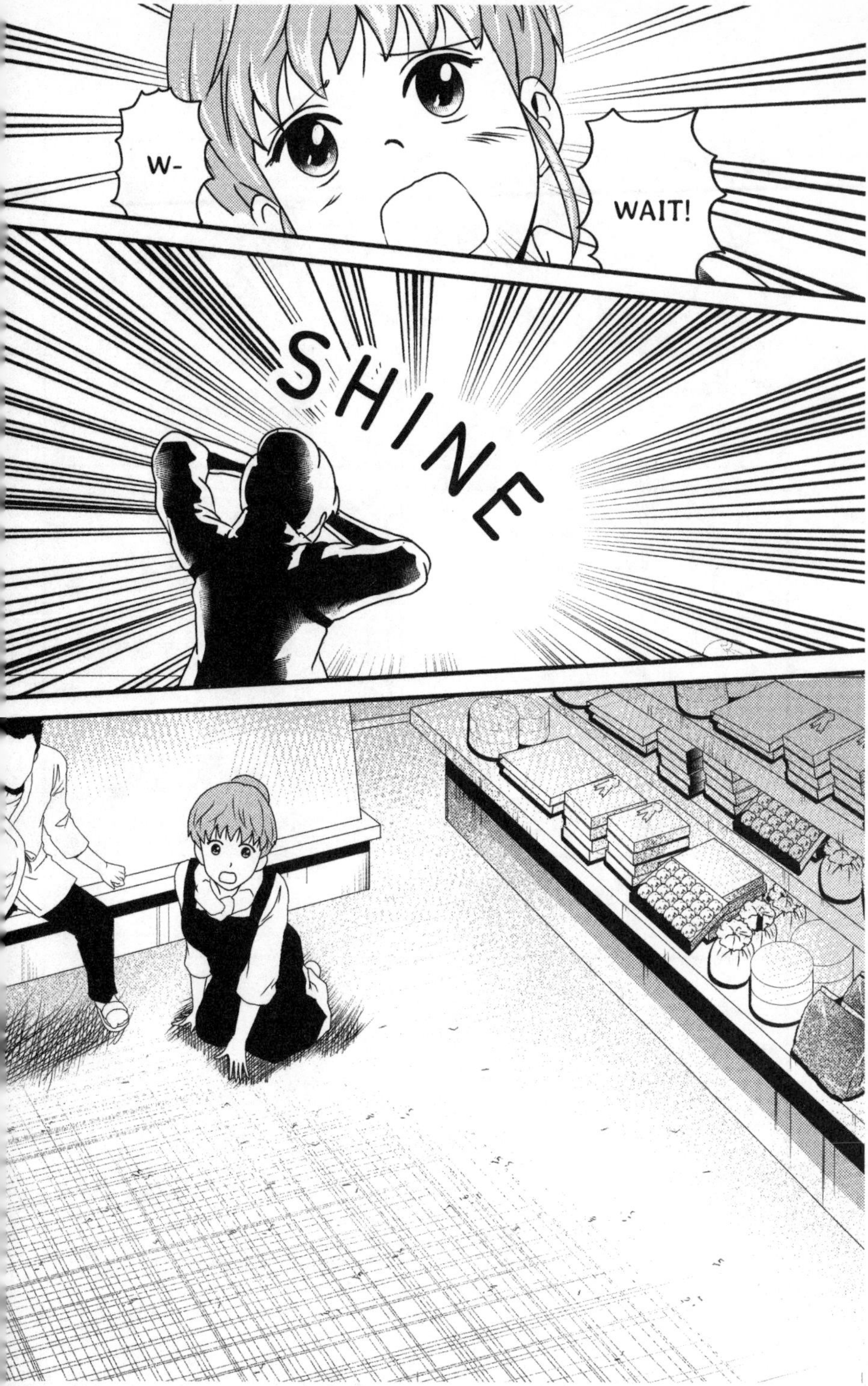
W-
WAIT!
SHINE

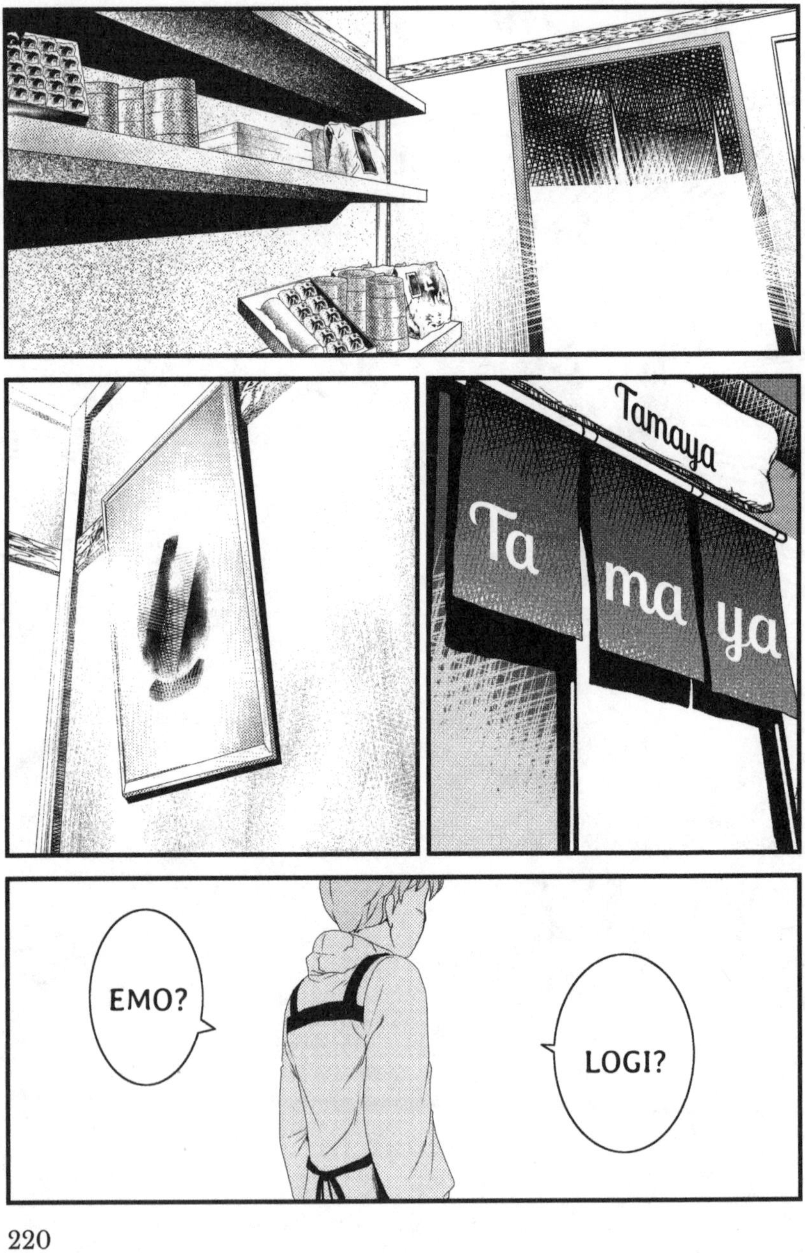
Tamaya
Ta ma ya
EMO?
LOGI?

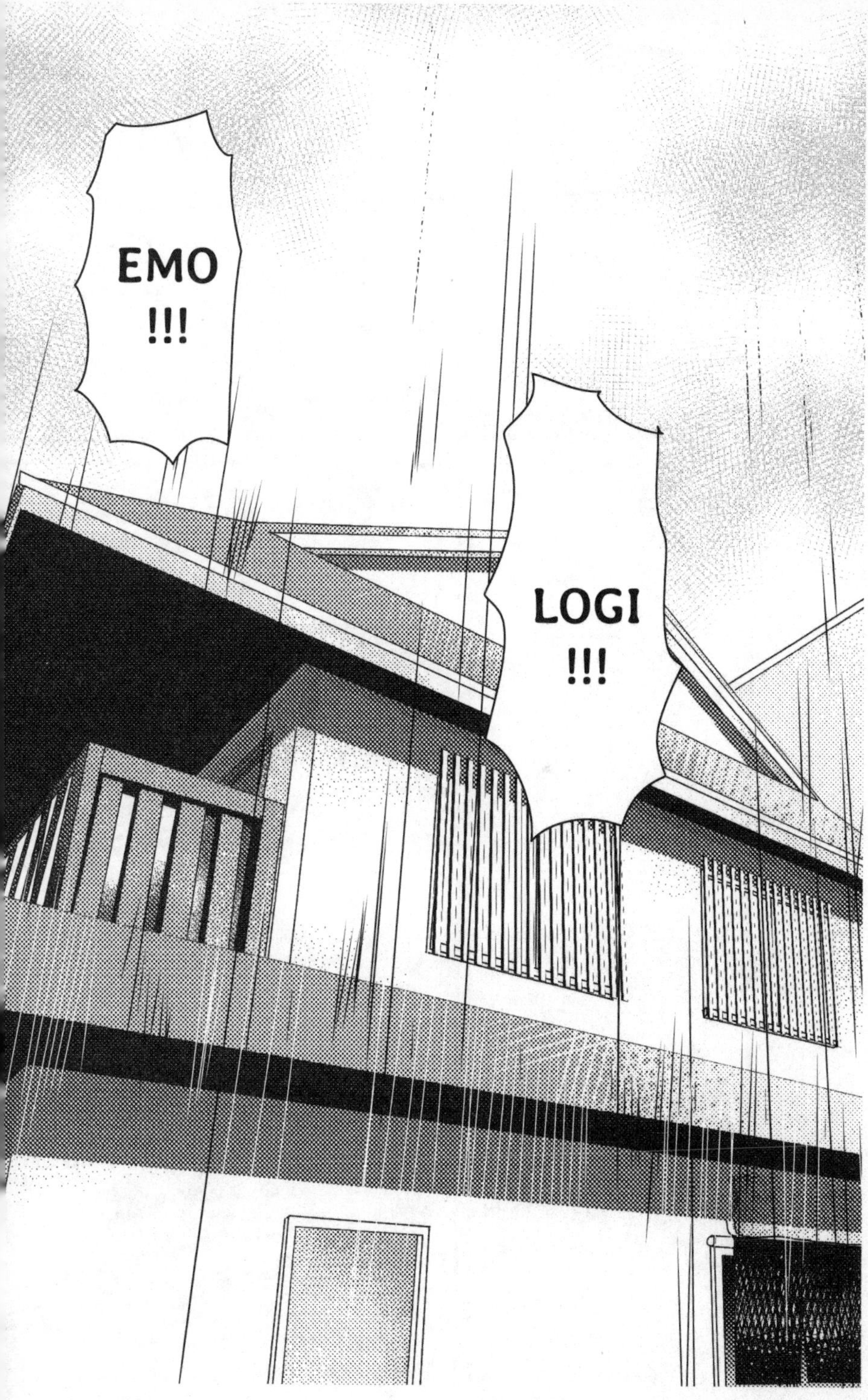
LOGI !!!
EMO !!!

A FEW MONTHS AFTER THAT

THIS IS THE MANJU FROM HOKKAIDO THAT EVERYONE'S BEEN TALKING ABOUT!

WE'LL BE INTRODUCING THEIR HOT NEW PRODUCT!

TAMAI...

... WONDERFUL JOB. THIS PROJECT IS APPROVED.

THANK YOU VERY MUCH!

CONGRATS!

DID SOMETHING HAPPEN THERE?

WOW! YOUR PROJECT WAS APPROVED!

YOU'VE REALLY CHANGED SINCE YOU CAME BACK FROM YOUR HOMETOWN.

HUH? NOTHING MUCH.

NOW, WE HAVE SOMEONE FROM THE SHOP TO TELL US MORE.

SINCE THOSE TWO MYSTERIOUS GUYS DISAPPEARED, THE NEW PRODUCT WE DEVELOPED TOGETHER STEADILY TURNED INTO A BIG HIT.

223

WE WERE ABLE TO MAKE PEOPLE ENJOY MANJU WITH OUR NEW PRODUCT, AND, AT THE SAME TIME, PEOPLE HAVE ALSO BEEN ENJOYING OUR OLD, TRADITIONAL MARIMO MANJU. THIS MAKES ME VERY HAPPY.

YES, THAT'S GREAT NEWS. DO YOU HAVE ANY GOALS FOR YOUR SHOP RIGHT NOW?

I'M HAPPIEST WHEN THE CUSTOMERS LIKE OUR PRODUCTS.

WE'LL KEEP MAKING THE SAME UNCHANGING MANJU FLAVOR WHILE KEEPING UP WITH THE CHANGING TIMES.

MARIMO, THIS IS YOUR FAMILY'S SHOP, RIGHT? IT'S BEEN ON TV THIS ENTIRE TIME! THAT'S AMAZING!

DAD ...

IT'S A MYSTERY WHY, BUT SOMEHOW I'M THE ONLY ONE WHO REMEMBERS THOSE TWO.

WE SHOULD CELEBRATE YOUR COMEBACK, MARIMO! LET'S GO DRINKING TODAY!

WAIT. JUST A BIT MORE.

OH, BUT DIDN'T YOU HAVE A DATE WITH YOUR BOY-FRIEND?

HE TOLD YOU HE WANTED TO GET BACK TOGETHER, RIGHT?

MARIMO...

I WANT TO START OVER WITH YOU.

WHA-AAT?!

YOU REJECTED HIM?!

WELL, HE'S GREAT, BUT...

...WHEN I THOUGHT ABOUT IT, BECAUSE OF THE THINGS HE SAID TO ME, EVEN IF WE GET BACK TOGETHER, I'LL PROBABLY ONLY GET MID-TERM SATISFACTION FROM THE RELATIONSHIP.

THE MID-TERM? MARIMO, YOU'VE REALLY CHANGED.

NAH, SOMEBODY JUST TAUGHT ME ABOUT THAT.

OH?

WHO?

A LIGHT AND DARK ANGEL.

HUH? WHAT?

NO, NEVER MIND.

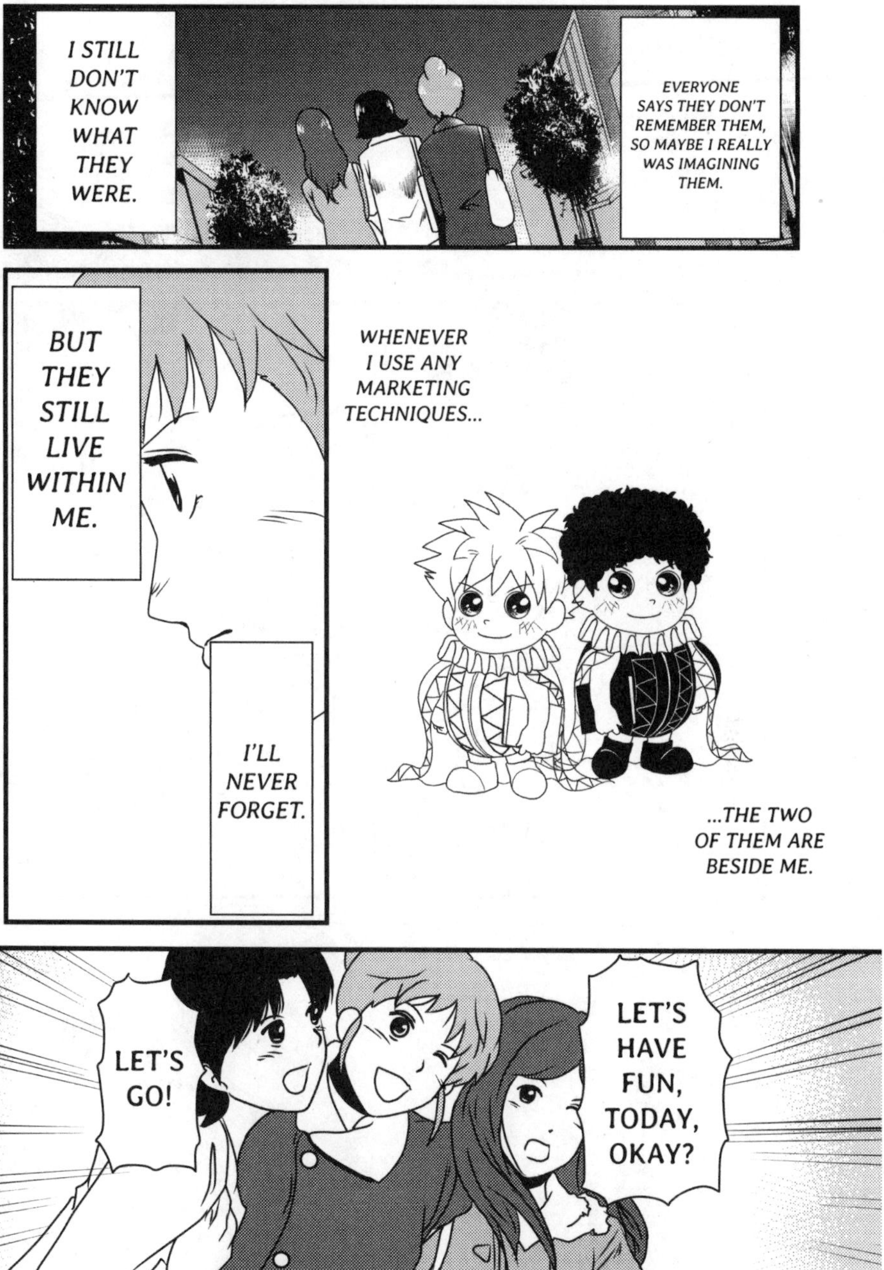
I STILL DON'T KNOW WHAT THEY WERE.
EVERYONE SAYS THEY DON'T REMEMBER THEM, SO MAYBE I REALLY WAS IMAGINING THEM.
BUT THEY STILL LIVE WITHIN ME.
I'LL NEVER FORGET.
WHENEVER I USE ANY MARKETING TECHNIQUES...
...THE TWO OF THEM ARE BESIDE ME.
LET'S GO!
LET'S HAVE FUN, TODAY, OKAY?

MEANWHILE, AT THEIR RIVAL, KIZA BAKERY...

WHA-AAT ?!

PAPA! WHAT DO YOU MEAN A BIG MANUFACTURER FROM THE MAINLAND LOOKING TO EXPAND HERE IS ACQUIRING OUR COMPANY?!

THAT'S RIGHT. IT'S A BIGGER BAKERY THAN WE ARE.

OH. THEY SAID THAT IF YOU AGREE TO MARRY THEIR DAUGHTER, THEY'LL SAVE OUR COMPANY.

MARRY?! THEY CAN'T JUST FORCE THAT!

NARUO. MARRY THIS GIRL.

WHA-AA?!

NOO-OOO!

TAMAYA HAS BEEN GARNERING POPULARITY BY OFFERING PRODUCTS THAT YOU CAN ENJOY WITH FAMILY AND FRIENDS, ALONG WITH THEIR TRADITIONAL SPECIALTY.

YOU CAN FEEL THE EARNESTNESS WITH WHICH THEY TRY TO UNDERSTAND THEIR CUSTOMER'S FEELINGS AND DEVELOP NEW PRODUCTS BASED ON THAT.

YES. WE'LL CONTINUE TO PROTECT THIS SHOP FOR 20 OR EVEN 30 MORE YEARS.

AND THAT'S IT FOR OUR SPECIAL FEATURE ON THE POPULAR TAMAYA!

The Importance of Capturing Your Customers

Customer satisfaction has been regarded as essential in doing business since ancient times. Customer satisfaction is viewed as even more important now that rival companies and products are everywhere. Satisfied customers will not only keep using your product or service, but will possibly spread good words about your product. On the other hand, unsatisfied customers will not use your product or service again. It's also possible that they will spread bad reviews of your product. It's a given that every customer's satisfaction is important, but the effect that a customer's satisfaction level can have on your sales has increased over the years.

Total sales from a single customer's use of a product or service over a lifetime is called **lifetime value**. It shows just how big an effect customer satisfaction can have on company sales. Satisfied customers will normally keep on using the same product or service. If they are satisfied enough, customers won't easily switch to another product or service. As a result, the accumulated sales from that customer will continue to increase through the years. The opposite is true for dissatisfied customers. A dissatisfied customer will use your product less and less and may eventually stop using it at all. As a result, the total sales for that customer will decrease. Various marketing strategies are necessary in order to maximize this lifetime value. Maximizing the lifetime value by increasing customer satisfaction is one of marketing's biggest challenges.

Lifetime Value Calculation

Customer Satisfaction

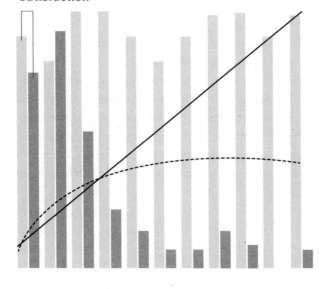

_____ Lifetime value when customer satisfaction is maintained

----- Lifetime value when customer satisfaction declines after a few years

Lifetime Value = Annual Transaction Value x Earning Rate x Retention Time in Years

To increase a customer's lifetime value, you need to establish a long-term relationship with that customer. This is greatly affected by how much a customer cares for and how they view their relationship with your company.

When a new customer is satisfied with your product, they will become a repeat customer and eventually will become a regular. If they grow to care even more about your company, they will become your supporter and be a voice for your company. The Customer Evolution chart on the next page looks at the stages of a customer's relationship with a company. **By building a good relationship with their customers, a company can increase their sales and maintain or increase their profits, which helps them keep growing.**

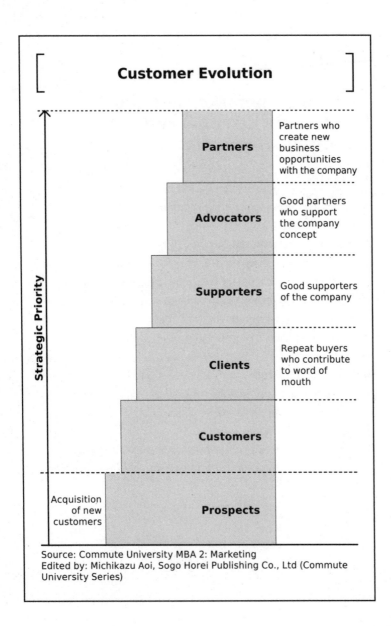

Customer Evolution

Strategic Priority

Partners — Partners who create new business opportunities with the company

Advocators — Good partners who support the company concept

Supporters — Good supporters of the company

Clients — Repeat buyers who contribute to word of mouth

Customers

Acquisition of new customers — **Prospects**

Source: Commute University MBA 2: Marketing
Edited by: Michikazu Aoi, Sogo Horei Publishing Co., Ltd (Commute University Series)

2

The Components of Customer Satisfaction: Essential and Nonessential Functions

In the Pyramid of Customer Satisfaction shown on the next page, the components that make up customer satisfaction are split into two types according to prior expectations.

First, we have the **essential functions** that the customer thinks of as musts for the product or service. These are functions and services they already know about and fully expect to receive. They are indispensable. Excessively improving these functions won't raise customer satisfaction by much, but if these functions fall below a certain standard, customer satisfaction will drop significantly.

Nonessential functions are functions and services that a customer is not expecting. Since they do not know about them beforehand, customers receiving them will be pleased.

To increase satisfaction, it's important to satisfy all essential functions and to increase and improve nonessential functions.

The Components and Pyramid of Customer Satisfaction

Functions	Customer Expectation	If met	If not met	Important point	Example (car)
Essential	Are musts for the customer and therefore expected	Not dissatisfied (not necessarily satisfied)	Dissatisfied	If any of these are missing, satisfaction drops significantly.	• Runs
Non-essential	Not seen as musts, and having these makes the customer happy	Increases satisfaction	Not satisfied (but not dissatisfied)	If any of these are met, satisfaction increases greatly.	• Brand image • Comfort

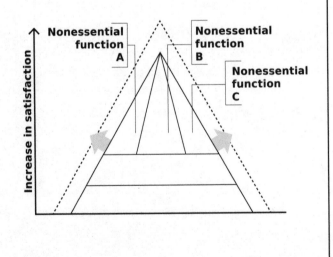

Take Good Care of Your Best Customers

The **80-20 principle** states that 80% of outcomes result from 20% of causes. It is also known as the 20-80 law, the 2:8 law, and the 80-20 rule, among others.

In business, it is often said that 80% of your sales (profit) come from the top 20% of your customers. Depending on the total number of customers and the product offered, this ratio can become 90-10 or 70-30, but the bigger your company's scope and the more customers you have, the closer this ratio gets to 80-20.

Applied to sales, this rule can also mean that 80% of your company's sales come from your top 20% of products.

A company's sales and profit come mostly from its hit products and top customers. By maintaining your relationships with your best customers who have the highest purchase frequency and the highest amount spent, you can maximize their lifetime value.

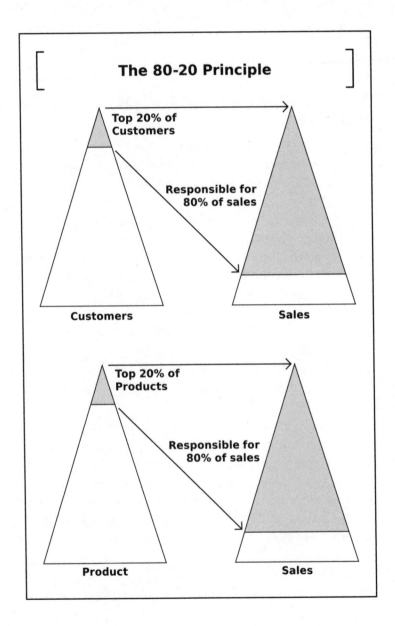

The 80-20 Principle

Top 20% of Customers

Responsible for 80% of sales

Customers

Sales

Top 20% of Products

Responsible for 80% of sales

Product

Sales

Why Is Customer Satisfaction Important?

Along with the 80-20 principle, there are several other rules that express how important customer satisfaction is. Two of the more popular ones are the 1-5 rule and the 5-25 rule.

The **1-5 rule** says that the cost for acquiring a new customer is five times that of maintaining an existing one. This is a well-known rule in industries that offer membership-based services and highly repeatable purchases. Existing customers have already experienced using the product and simple sales promotion methods like direct mail or a sale are enough to greatly increase the probability of a repeat purchase. On the other hand, since new customers have never used the product or service before, you will need to use more aggressive sales promotions with them, such as offering large discounts or sample products for free.

The **5-25 rule** says that a 5% improvement in customer retention will lead to at least a 25% increase in revenue. This rule also applies to membership services and repeatable purchases. If you can improve your customer retention for existing customers, you can avoid not only the cost of acquiring a new customer as stated in the 1-5 rule, but you can also avoid all the one-time transaction and sales management costs. Since you can also expect some positive reviews, an improvement in customer retention could greatly improve your revenue.

Knowing these customer satisfaction rules and understanding how much a repeat purchase from a satisfied customer can affect your revenue can help you see the path through one of marketing's most important challenges.

Rules Related to Customer Satisfaction

Rule	Description
1-5 Rule	The cost of acquiring one new customer is five times the cost of maintaining an existing one. This is particularly relevant for industries that offer membership systems and highly repeatable purchases.
5-25 Rule	If you improve customer retention by 5%, you can improve revenue by at least 25%. This rule highlights the importance of maintaining your existing customers.

References

- "Kotler's Marketing Concept," by Philip Kotler, translated by Naoto Onzo and Shuji Okawa, Toyo Keizai Inc.
- "Marketing Management," by Philip Kotler, supervised by Shoji Murata, translated by Jo Kosaka, Yumiko Mimura, and Satoshi Hikita, President, Inc.
- "Marketing Principles," by Philip Kotler and Gary Armstrong, translated by Mitsuo Wada, President, Inc.
- The Strategy of Competition, Newly revised, by M. E. Porter, translated by Kun Toki, Teruo Hattori, and Manji Nakatsuji, Diamond Inc.
- The Strategy of Competitive Advantage, M. E. Porter, translated by Kun Toki, Diamond Inc.
- "Strategic Market Management," D. A. Aker, Ikujiro Nonaka, Tadahiro Kitahora, Mitsuteru Shimaguchi, Junzo Ishii, Diamond Inc.
- "Creative Imitation Strategy," Stephen P. Schnarz, Naoto Onzo, Kazue Shimamura, Tomoaki Banno, Yuhikaku Co.
- "Marketing Strategy," Stephen P. Schnarz, translated by Manabu Uchida and Yosuke Yamamoto, PHP Research Institute, Inc.
- "Introduction to Seminar Marketing," by Junzo Ishii, Mitsuteru Shimaguchi, Qi Kuriki, and Takuro Yoda, Nikkei Inc.

- "Introduction to Seminar Marketing," by Junzo Ishii, Mitsuteru Shimaguchi, Qi Kuriki, and Takuro Yoda, Nikkei Inc.
- The Strategic Logic of Brand Elements, edited by Naoto Onzo and Akihiro Kamei, Waseda University Press
- "Simple Marketing, Revised Edition," by Yukio Mori, Softbank Creative Inc.
- Basic Knowledge of Management Terms, edited by Nomura Research Institute, Diamond Inc.
- "The Work of a Marketer," Fumihiko Kojima, JMA Management Center, Inc.
- "60 Minute Kigyo Dantotsuka Project," by Masanori Kanda, Diamond Inc.
- "MBA Marketing," by Dallas Murphy, translated by Mitsuteru Shimaguchi and Akiki Yoshikawa, Nikkei Inc.
- "The Marketing Class I Wish I'd Taken Earlier," by Manabu Uchida and Naoya Ito, PHP Research Institute, Inc.
- "Marketing," by Global Task Force, supervised by Michikazu Aoi, Sogo-Joho Shuppan, Inc.
- Marketing Ga Wakaru Jiten (Dictionary of Marketing), written by Tokuhiro Tanabe, published by Nihon Jitsugyo Shuppansha, Ltd.
- "The World's Easiest-to-Understand Book on Marketing," by Takashi Yamashita, East Press, Inc.
- "The Art of Psychological Marketing," by Shuji Shigeta, PHP Research Institute.
- Various materials and business books, including documents for seminars at IVC
- Various other Internet sites

Author's Profile
Takashi Yasuda

After graduating from the Faculty of Science and Engineering, Takashi Yasuda worked in marketing research and consulting before joining a mail order company as a merchandising advisor and marketing manager. He contributed to the company's growth by branding the products it handled and implementing sales promotion measures that led to an increase in annual sales of several hundred million yen. Later, at an Internet shopping company, he was in charge of improving operations and business efficiency in order to expand business.

Currently, he participates in IVC, which builds information that changes the value of things and the infrastructure that provides that information. He is engaged in consulting and new business development for a variety of clients.

His areas of expertise range from the development of marketing and PR strategies tailored to the field to the launch of mail order businesses. He also conducts seminars, lectures, and writes articles on how to utilize marketing in the field.

His motto is " 行雲流水 " which means "to be as free as the clouds and water."

He is the author of *Hajimete Manabu Marketing no Hon* (The First Book of Marketing), published by JMA Management Center, among others.

yasuda@intelligence-value.com